Praise for *The Insightful L*

"Levick and Bertman have crafted a leader's field book with *The Insightful Leader*, laying out the road map to fostering a sense of ownership for those you lead, while creating a culture for courage, success, and enrichment. A must-read for every leader and every leader to be."

—**Mark Davidoff,** retired Michigan managing partner,
Deloitte; president and CEO, The Fisher Group

"*The Insightful Leader* offers a transformative approach to leadership that puts employees at the heart of organizational success. By shifting perspective to view leadership through employees' eyes, readers will discover powerful strategies to create a thriving, innovative workplace."

—**Dr. Brian Doane,** MD, FACEP, assistant medical director,
Northwest Community Hospital

"This book helps people understand much more clearly why it is so important for any leader to lead with a clear sense of emotional intelligence. It is not just a catchphrase but a 'must-do' for all leaders. In fact, it's a must-read for every type of leader."

—**Paul Ray,** president, Ilmor Engineering

"This book offers a compelling perspective on leadership and self-reflection, helping today's leaders navigate evolving workplace dynamics. By encouraging leaders to confront challenging topics head-on and engaging with the next generation of workers, this book provides valuable insights, fostering positive change that can improve personal performance and overall well-being."

—**Chandra Madafferi,** president and CEO,
Michigan Education Association

"Why did no one tell me all this years ago—or, more accurately, why did I not think to look for this before starting my leadership career? This is a compelling and easy read, matching my experience and convictions in so many ways. The authors' exemplary vulnerability is on show throughout this book populated with memorable and relatable real-life examples that made me laugh out loud. The teachings and lessons to be learned here are essential for good leadership. Take note!"

—**Neil Armstrong,** chief people officer, Mercedes-Benz Research and Development, North America

"Everyone in a leadership role in the business world has been exposed to dozens of books and seminars concerning leadership. For most such people, a dulling sameness took over long ago. What typically remains unaddressed in this vast sea of information is anything that offers the potential for breakthrough results while being practical enough to deploy in daily life. What a pleasant surprise to find, in this fast-paced book, a jarring exception to this uninspiring predicament.

The Insightful Leader gives the reader the foundation for a fundamental reassessment and recalibration of their management practices. Sometimes the introspection that thereby arises can be a bit painful, but it's well worth it. I don't know of any book about leadership or management that I would recommend in lieu of this one. I wish it had been written years ago."

—**Gary Pearce,** former chief risk, compliance and privacy officer, Kelly Services, Inc.

"Congratulations to Dr. Keith and Matt for authoring a powerful strategic management book. The text provides valuable insights for leaders facing challenges in all areas related to being successful. As experts on work culture and human behavior, they effectively identify and manage these aspects within organizations. This book smartly addresses how to understand better leadership skills that lead to organizational success. Dr. Keith and Matt strike a balanced tone, offering meaningful, actionable information rather than just another leadership book."

—**William V. Taylor,** president and CEO, Delaware Compensation Rating Bureau and Pennsylvania Compensation Rating Bureau

"A must-read for ALL leaders of people! Keith and Matt go where no one has ever gone by asking if you would fire your boss. All leaders ask themselves "What do direct reports think of me?" Yet, few leaders create a culture or environment to solicit honest feedback! This book examines the disconnect between a leader's actions and intentions while exposing blind spots they need to be mindful of to create trust and drive performance. Bravo!"

—Joseph R. Hurshe, FACHE, president and CEO,
Munson Medical Center

"Self-awareness is what separates a truly effective leader from those who simply possess a title. *The Insightful Leader* provides leaders with valuable tools for understanding what motivates employees in order to earn their commitment. An empowering read. Highly recommended!"

—David McNally, CPAE, founder and CEO, TransForm Corporation;
best-selling author, *Be Your Own Brand* and *If You're Alive*

"*The Insightful Leader* recognizes that great technicians make up the pool in which most companies find leaders. Rarely do you find leaders who have been educated in leadership theory and/or philosophy that can fuse individualized leadership skills. *The Insightful Leader* provides a practical bridge to give those great technicians, who have innate leadership talent, specific tools and insights to build or refine a robust, successful leadership practice. Most leaders won't incur the humility of failed leadership, nor incur the cost of graduate degrees; and most companies won't provide endless time to overcome the learning curve of great leadership. As a result, 60 percent of employees dream of their leader's departure. Dr. Keith and Matt have created a "super tool" for every leader's toolbox to help give those great technicians a richer path to being an insightful leader."

—Eric L. Spencer, president and CEO, Arbitration Forums

"Dr. Keith Levick and Matt Bertman provide incredible and astonishing insight into how employees view their leaders. They establish our blind spots as managers, the urgency for us to have a paradigm shift from manager to coach, and the requirement for employees to have meaning and purpose in their work. This book must be read by all people in a leadership role so they can connect and form a bond with those on the team they serve."

—**Emmanuel E. Manuelidis,** senior vice president and chief claims officer, H.W. Kaufman Group

"*The Insightful Leader* flips the script and curiously looks at the voice of the employee in defining what good leadership looks like. And the employee vote declares 60 percent would fire their manager. There may be no bigger headwind with regard to an organization activating its strategy and achieving its full potential than the disconnect between the employee and manager. Levick and Bertman provide a fresh perspective on an ageless challenge and a tangible road map for success."

—**Brad Haudan,** president, Root, an Accenture company

"A treasure trove of solid and tremendously useful information and guidance for anyone currently in a leadership position, as well as those who aspire to be. I only wish this valuable book had been around much earlier in my own career!"

—**Jan Berris,** vice president, National Committee on United States-China Relations

The Insightful Leader

DISCOVER YOUR BLIND SPOTS
THROUGH THE EYES OF EMPLOYEES

Keith Levick, PhD & Matt Bertman, MA

RIVER GROVE
BOOKS

Published by River Grove Books
Austin, TX
www.rivergrovebooks.com

Distributed by River Grove Books

Design and composition by Greenleaf Book Group
Cover design by Greenleaf Book Group
Graphics created with Build-a-Graphic and Presentation Process
Cover images used under license from ©Adobestock.com

Publisher's Cataloging-in-Publication data is available.

Print ISBN: 978-1-63299-927-6

eBook ISBN: 978-1-63299-928-3

First Edition

KEITH'S DEDICATIONS

I would like to acknowledge several people who supported me during the writing of this book. First and foremost, my loving and patient wife, Debbie. Her tolerance and emotional support were invaluable. My children, Lisa Levick-Doane and her husband Brian, and Brad and his wife Allison; and my four fantastic grandchildren, Molly, Eli, Matthew, and Leah.

Additionally, Dr. Alan Hoffman was my advisor and mentor when I completed my doctoral work years ago. The insight and expertise that he imparted to me are forever etched in my brain.

Finally, Mrs. Jane Raitt, my senior-year high school English teacher, who inspired me to read and become a critical thinker. She created confidence in me, and she became a motivating force to pursue my academic journey. May her memory be a blessing.

MATT'S DEDICATIONS

Thank you to my wife, Michel, who has witnessed my passion for leadership throughout my career beginning as early as our undergraduate evening study dates in the library at Michigan State University. For my children Jordyn, Joshua, and Andrew, your generational insights have taught me new perspectives on leadership and, more importantly, how to apply those corporate leadership lessons to fatherhood! As each of you begin the early stages of professional careers, may the leadership lessons within this book help serve as a guide for success.

To my parents, Dr. Stephen and Elaine Bertman, who each in their careers served in the field of education as lifelong educators teaching me the value and importance of learning. Specifically, to my father who has authored countless articles, essays, and books, thank you for all the leadership newspaper clippings you shared with me over the years and reinforcing within me how the importance of Greek and Roman wisdom and history can serve as valuable leadership lessons in today's modern society.

To my writing partner, Dr. Keith Levick, thank you for your countless hours of leadership coaching and always challenging and encouraging me to bring my full self to our "writer's meetings."

Finally, to all those colleagues who I have worked with over the years. Hopefully I have demonstrated many of the various leadership qualities found throughout this book and made a memorable impact on those I've had the pleasure and honor to have coached and led.

Contents

Introduction

Writing a fresh book on leadership is daunting for several reasons, the first being the sheer volume of material on this topic in circulation today. A quick Amazon search reveals nearly 60,000 books with the word "leadership" in the title.

Despite this overwhelming number, a fundamental problem exists in many of the leadership books we read. Most tend to fall into one of two categories. They are either written from the perspective of someone who has proved themselves to be an exceptional leader in their field, or from the vantage point of someone who simply possesses expertise on the topic. For example, a well-respected athlete excels at their craft, so they write a book on leadership. Or a leadership guru has studied the subject of leadership ad nauseam and approaches their writing from theory, with little personal experience to back up their approach. This is not to say that those who have demonstrated principles of leadership don't have insights and perspectives; instead, sometimes those best served to provide insight have witnessed the behaviors and actions of leaders as opposed to being in the role themselves.

The major problem with leadership today is perspective. As Stephen Covey said, "We see others through their actions and ourselves through our intentions."[1] Deep down, very few leaders recognize this disconnect. These leaders know there are blind spots they need to change and ways they could improve their leadership.

With this in mind, we investigated what direct reports say they genuinely need and want from their leaders. (We use the term *direct report* instead of *employee*.) During a period of four years, we created a twelve-question survey and distributed it at two different points in time to fifty randomly selected diverse companies (small, medium, and large) across the United States. We received over five hundred responses from employees on each survey.

We entered our survey with four guiding hypotheses. First, direct reports generally hold back and will not share their honest feelings with their boss. Second, bosses do not know what their direct reports honestly think of them. Third, direct reports would terminate their boss if they could. And fourth, direct reports would sacrifice something intrinsically or extrinsically crucial in exchange for their boss being fired. Some examples of intrinsic sacrifices would include vacation days (work-life harmony) or promotions (having a meaningful career). Those extrinsic examples would include more monetary examples such as salary and bonus.

This survey provided startling results, providing leaders with new and refreshing information, which we describe throughout this book. In this way, we believe *The Insightful Leader* is different from most leadership books. Instead of supplying our own *wisdom*, we thought it would be more enlightening to let you see leaders through the actual words of the people who work for them. We found the responses so authentic that we chose some of our personal favorites and placed them at the start of each chapter.

This book is targeted for all leaders, including those who manage direct reports, team leaders, and even those employees who aspire to become leaders—in companies of all sizes, from small family businesses to nonprofit organizations to large Fortune 500 companies.

The first section of chapters in the book will discuss the survey responses and feedback, while the remaining chapters will focus on the most significant blind spots of a leader. In these chapters, you will find common mistakes leaders make and techniques and skills you can use to improve your skill set. As you begin to engage with this book, we encourage you to take off your blindfold, accept the feedback, and gain insight rarely seen by those in your leadership position.

THE NEED FOR INSIGHTFUL LEADERSHIP

CHAPTER 1

Would You Fire Your Boss?

In a heartbeat!

"Would you fire your boss?" This question added significance to our research following the survey we conducted in 2020 of over five hundred employees. In that questionnaire, we asked everyone this pointed question: "If at some point you were given the opportunity, would you fire your boss?"

The results were startling. Of the 521 employees who responded, a startling 44 percent stated they would fire their boss if they had the opportunity. Of those who responded, 42 percent were from companies with between 2 and 99 employees; 31 percent were from companies with 100 to 999 employees; and 27 percent were from companies with 1000 or more employees. Sixty-one percent were females, and 39 percent were males.

Here are some enlightening responses from the survey:

- 41 percent indicated their boss (which we termed a supervisor or manager) cared little about their opinion.

- 46 percent stated their boss seldom, if ever, admits their mistakes.

- 31.5 percent said their boss seldom, if ever, recognizes their accomplishments.

- 32 percent noted that their boss did not collaboratively work with them.

- 44 percent said their boss did not take the time to learn the personal aspects of their life.

- 44 percent said they would have fired their boss at some point if given the opportunity.

- 60 percent would forego something of value to fire their boss.

The last two bullet points are the most significant. Of that 44 percent, we asked a direct follow-up question: "What would you give up for one year in exchange for seeing your boss fired?" Again, the responses were astounding. Twenty-two percent said they would forego some vacation time, 13 percent voted for a decrease in salary, and 25 percent indicated they would forego a potential promotion. In other words, 60 percent of participants said they would give up something valuable to see their boss fired!

After working as consultants in and with human resources (HR) for decades, we both knew there would be a certain number of disgruntled employees in these organizations who felt undervalued by their employers. However, 44 percent was eye-opening.

What was more startling—something that, as researchers and authors of this book, neither of us could have anticipated or predicted—came four years later when we asked the same questions in 2024.

In the past couple of years, post-pandemic research regarding employees and their work lives has continued to shake up the landscape of the work environment as we historically know it. With this in mind, we wondered if the results from the initial survey we took in the spring of 2020 were affected—changed—by the pandemic. After all, everyone's lives were affected in some way or another. To answer our question, we decided to send out the same survey questions that were in our first survey to another random group of organizations and employees in 2024. We replicated the same process and qualifiers.

Initially, we hypothesized that the second survey would yield different results. We thought, for example, that fewer people would want to fire their boss. Since COVID-19 was behind us, workplaces have adjusted to the changes that resulted from the pandemic. As with any two professionals brainstorming, alternative thoughts emerged. Have employees and organizations accepted the hybrid model and other significant workplace changes?

The results of Survey II answered our questions. The 529 responses mirrored the results from the first survey in almost every question and category but one. In Survey I (2020), 44 percent of respondents said they would fire their boss. But in Survey II (2024), a whopping 60 percent of respondents would show their bosses to the door! That was approximately a 30 percent increase in respondents from the previous survey confirming they wanted to fire their boss!

The reasons given were varied. The top issues noted were the boss's desire to avoid conflict and difficult conversations. Along with this was mistrust, hesitancy to provide ongoing coaching, ineffective management styles, an inability to provide open and honest feedback, and being a poor listener. When it came down to it, participants felt their bosses were ineffective and untrustworthy in their management styles.

Oh, If I Could Make My Boss Disappear

This revelation reminded us of the 1980 hit comedy film *9 to 5*, starring Dolly Parton, Lily Tomlin, and Jane Fonda. For those of you whose memories do not date back that far, the plot of this movie revolved around three female secretaries who decided to get revenge on their tyrannical, sexist boss by abducting him and running the business themselves. And yes, it is just as ridiculous as it sounds!

In a dramatic sequence of events, these three women pounce on an opportune moment when their boss has a bad fall in their office, banging his head on the desk and collapsing unconscious on the floor. Seeing this as their chance, they kidnap him and keep him locked up at his home—along the way collecting enough evidence of his fraudulent actions so they can blackmail him into silence.

Oddly enough, while these three women have their boss abducted and confined to his own home, productivity in the company skyrockets! When they finally allow him to return, the senior leaders in the organization offer him a promotion and company transfer to Brazil—effectively removing him from their lives forever.[1]

Again, it's a crazy narrative, but it resonates with audiences for a reason. Deep down inside, 44 percent of participants in 2020 and 60 percent from the survey in 2024 secretly wish they could see their bosses magically disappear.

It's the reason movies like *Horrible Bosses* are a hit. It's why outlandish characters such as Michael Scott in *The Office* are both adored and hated. Laying the comedy angle aside, there is a part of characters like this that rings true in the workplace. These outlandish characters resonate with us not because we admire their qualities, but because we have fallen prey to some of the same nonprofessional behavior they display.

Anyone who has taken a psychology course learns that an over-inflated ego is a common weakness in people. A leader's sense of self-importance can derail their ability to establish and maintain a strong relationship with their direct report.

The Cost of Ego

Blind spots often occur in the leader's line of sight in their desperation to climb the corporate ladder. This, in turn, enhances the risk of developing and perpetuating an inflated ego. As leaders continue to be promoted throughout their careers, they are often more secluded and insulated from people on the lower end of the ladder. The high altitude can blind their vision, distorting the organization's culture and people, thus continuing to fuel their ego.

Regardless of what rung of the ladder you stand on, your ego stands with you. As you advance, you acquire more power. And if ego is defined as a sense of self-importance, then power can only inflate this. A self-inflated ego combined with power is a recipe for being blinded from meeting your direct reports' needs.

There are many forms of power found in society and the workplace. With our focus on the workplace, three types of power typically manifest: *positional*, *ascribed*, and *personal*.

Positional power is the authority that comes with a specific role. For example, you are the VP of Sales, and with that position comes certain privileges others do not share.

Ascribed power is how much power comes to you from the people who work with you. It has nothing to do with your position in the organization. Examples of this are found when you become the answer person in the department. Or, due to your dynamic and charismatic personality, people are drawn to you. In other words, they ascribe power to you.

Personal power refers to how you perceive yourself. It is your self-esteem and self-worth, which are the critical elements of your ego.

We often ask participants in our workshops this question: If you had your choice of only one of the three types of power, which one would you pick? Most people select either ascribed or personal power. On the surface, this makes sense. But then we take the discussion to the next level with the following belief: If you had a great deal of personal power, people would be drawn to you (ascribed power), and with personal and ascribed power, chances are your promotion possibilities would increase.

Consider the converse. Think about the worst leader you ever reported to. What made them such poor leaders? Chances are they were micromanagers, had trouble connecting with you, or their personal power was weak.

An interesting observation has crystallized over many years of coaching and training leaders. Leaders with weak *personal* power often abuse their *positional* power. Anecdotally, we have seen this play out in organizations. Society has many examples, as seen by politicians and other professionals who abuse their positional power. Upon closer examination, one wonders about the strength of one's ego.

In the book *Egonomics: What Makes Ego Our Greatest Asset (or Most Expensive Liability)* by David Marcum and Steven Smith, the authors discovered that "51 percent of businesspeople estimate that ego costs their company anywhere from 6 percent to 15 percent of annual revenue."[2]

According to Paul Nutt, over "one-third of all failed business decisions are driven by ego. Nearly two-thirds of executives never explore alternatives once they make up their minds. [And] 81 percent of managers push their decisions through by persuasion or edict, not by the relevance of their ideas."[3] The cost of ego is high.

Why They Leave

You might be familiar with that famous quote from best-selling author and management consultant Marcus Buckingham: "People don't leave companies; they leave their managers."[4] The question that seldom follows that statement is, "Why?" Why do people leave their leaders (managers or leaders)?

Answers vary among those who have moved on to greener pastures; however, some common threads weave through every response. In this book, we want to uncover why direct reports leave an organization and offer some robust solutions that will help you gain insight from your direct reports' perspectives.

If you are or aspire to be a high-performing leader, this book is for you. By following some of the proven principles in these pages, you can become someone who lives ahead of the game. You can avoid the pitfalls so many leaders stumble on along their journey. You can act with a high level of authenticity and cultural awareness, and you will anticipate obstacles on the horizon before others around you see them. You can become the boss your direct reports would never want to fire!

Insights

Your direct reports want you to . . .

- use your personal power to augment your positional and ascribed power.

- always check your ego at the door.

- care about their opinion and not be afraid to make mistakes.

CHAPTER 2

Lead Through Your Employees' Eyes

Have her walk a day in my shoes
to see what I do daily.

The reason we have so many poor bosses in positions of management today is because our system of promotion is flawed. Here is the problem. Many leaders enter new roles *not* because of superior leadership skills but because they have excelled at their *technical skills*; in other words, they are great *doers*. This is critical to understand.

Many CEOs' unfortunate assumption is that if someone on their team excels in one area, they can plug that individual in to a new role and expect similar high-performance results. But this is seldom the case. While someone might be an effective leader, this does not mean they will be a great leader. Frequently, leaders get promoted because of their technical acumen. Too often, managers are strong individual contributors who have caught the attention of senior management and are trusted in leadership positions.

Dr. John Kotter, author and emeritus at the Harvard Business School, points out people typically become managers because they are good technicians, have seniority, or know the right people.[1] Direct reports who have performed well in their jobs often receive increased compensation or are rewarded for good technical performance. Those who have put in their years of service are rewarded for longevity and loyalty. On occasion, organizational savvy or internal politics can play a role in career advancement, as it is often the case that it's not *what* we know but *who* we know. Not to mention the ever-present internal company politics.

John Doe might be a terrific sales rep and perform well in his role at work. But as good as John might be at sales, this does not provide a solid measurement of his future leadership performance. John may excel at *making the sale*, but that doesn't necessarily mean he will enjoy the administrative aspect of managing and motivating a sales force.

Why Bosses and Direct Reports View the World Differently

In 2016, *The Economist Executive Education Navigator* surveyed ". . . professionals that showed a significant difference between what executives think they need compared to what their employees wanted them to improve. In fact . . . the C-suite executives identified technology and finance that needed to improve. Whereas, employees wished their executives would strengthen EQ and become insightful leaders."[2]

This research not only underscores the importance of this book, but it speaks to how many leaders tend to lack self-awareness and overall social-emotional intelligence. This gets us to the heart of the matter. Most leadership books available today typically address areas and techniques related to communication, coaching and developing people, and other skills and behaviors that lead to success. But despite the vast resources at our disposal, developing highly effective leaders remains a challenge for most organizations. We believe this is the case for several reasons. For starters, most leaders *believe* they do a good job. Or, as longtime Florida Steel CEO Edward L. Flom famously stated, "One of the hardest tasks of leadership is understanding that you are not what you are, but what you're perceived to be by others."[3] Consequently, many leaders do not think they need to further their professional development and, thus, they remain blind to that necessity.

Leadership is a constant evolution. However, the danger is when leaders consistently switch their styles, techniques, and philosophies, like flavors of the month. It's OK to be encouraged to evolve your leadership style; however, be cautious not to bounce around from one philosophy to another like a golfer constantly trying to change their swing based on reacting to short-term outcomes.

Perhaps most concerning is how some corporate cultures are obsessed with the bottom line. Many organizations tend to focus on short-term financial results instead of long-term outcomes. As an example, we have seen companies cancel training opportunities to reduce costs to achieve a quarterly financial goal as opposed to recognizing the value and importance of developing their talent to meet a longer-term business objective. This behavior might satisfy the CEO and Board of Directors, but this shortsightedness can lead to unintended consequences—often resulting in leaders doing whatever it takes to maximize immediate profits while losing sight of the bigger picture.[4] When the mindset of a company shifts to focusing on leadership behaviors (things that can be modified and changed), it will lead to a higher return on investment and long-term success.

The default belief for many bosses is that the bottom line is all that matters. So long as there are no major team blowups, everything will be OK. Direct reports see the world quite differently. They feel the constant weight of a boss who lacks awareness. It is not something they can dismiss or ignore because it lingers with them . . . every . . . single . . . day.

The most significant advantage you have for being the best leader you can be rests in seeing through your direct reports' eyes.

Nearsighted View

Consider this example we often use in our workshops. As quickly as you can, read the following statement. After reading this statement, without taking additional time to think it over, count how many times the letter *F* is found in this statement:

> FINISHED FILES ARE THE RE-
> SULT OF YEARS OF SCIENTIF-
> IC STUDY COMBINED WITH
> THE EXPERIENCE OF MANY.

How many Fs did you discover as you read? Typically, when we conduct this exercise, the number of Fs counted in the sentence ranges from three to five. Is that what you counted? If so, you would be incorrect.

The actual number of Fs in this short paragraph is six! Feel free to go back and check, paying particular attention to the three OFs. Now, do you see them? If so, congratulations. Don't be frustrated. Roughly a mere 10 percent of participants see all six Fs the first time they look!

This begs the question, why are OFs so easy to overlook? One reason is that people tend to overlook prepositions in a sentence. Another reason has to do with how the brain interprets the word *of*. When you say the word out loud, the *of* sounds like an *ov*, allowing the brain to miss the word *of*.

What's interesting is to observe the strong beliefs formed in the individual who sees only three to five Fs. We often have fun and take this activity to the next level to drive home learning points. We suggest that there are more than three or four on their sheet of paper and that they reread the sentence to be sure of their answer. In most cases, they are more adamant about their original answer. When asked if they want to wager that they are wrong, they bet on credit cards, money, their computer, a watch, etc. When they realize that the entire class had the same sentence and they missed all or some of the *of*s, they sheepishly sink into their chairs with laughter. But, when we highlight the learning points of how the brain interprets the word *of* and, more importantly, how our perceptions (seeing only three Fs) drive behavior (wagering), the discussion becomes dynamic.

The person who can only see three Fs is like the boss who cannot see through their direct report's lens. When this happens, consider the impact this might have. They are blinded to the whole person—their needs, desires, passions, interests, etc.—just as we demonstrated someone having a blind spot in counting the Fs. Insightful leaders are less myopic and remain open-minded to their direct reports' perceptions, thoughts, and feelings.

Leveling the Playing Field

The term *employee* can sometimes carry a lot of baggage and even a sense of ownership. "You are *my* employee. My guy . . ." This thinking can cause leaders to refer to people as underlings and give the idea that they are somehow less in rank. Like how *employee* is replaced by *direct report*, the term *manager* or *supervisor* has been replaced with *leader*. Another term, *subordinate*, is also used in today's vernacular. A leader often refers to an employee as their *subordinate*. I don't know about you, but I don't want to be a *sub*ordinate to anyone. In fact, if you refer to someone like that, you are most likely setting yourself up for them to respond insubordinately.

We recalled coaching a high-potential leader who had recently been promoted. This gentleman was placed in a new role where he didn't have the functional expertise, he'd had in previous roles but was given this role in an effort to prepare him for future leadership positions. As it turned out, one of his most significant areas of development was the ability to empower his direct reports and allow them to serve as subject matter experts. Unfortunately, being somewhat insecure in his new role, this leader chose to constantly shield his direct reports from meetings, interactions, and involvement with senior leadership, to demonstrate he was more knowledgeable than all of them based on his newly appointed title and role.

As leaders, we must remind ourselves that we are role models.

We must model the desired behaviors we are looking to get from our direct reports. These behaviors can take shape in many ways; for example, you can symbolically communicate a strong message to your direct reports. An example we often like to share is when co-author Keith Levick took over a company from the previous owner after the owner retired. Keith needed to expand the office space and decided to clean out the rooms used for storage, which included two offices and a bathroom. We came in during a slow time in December to clean out and organize the backspace. Everyone selected a job to do. Dr. Keith, as he's known, purposely decided to pick first and chose to clean the bathroom and toilet. Envision what a toilet looks like that hasn't been used in over three years! You can't imagine the filth. The team saw him scrubbing that bathroom on his hands and knees, making it as clean as possible. Dr. Keith chose that dirty job purposefully. Symbolically, he wanted to send the message that there wasn't a job he would ask of his team that he wouldn't be willing to take on himself.

Another example of leveling the playing field is when Lee Iacocca, former chairman of the Chrysler Corporation, voluntarily limited his salary to $1 in September 1979. In a financial crisis and at risk of declaring bankruptcy, Iacocca led by example and demonstrated that he would take that cut rather than asking others to reduce their salaries.

If leadership is defined as getting work done through the efforts of others, then John Maxwell had it right in his book when he said, "Your people don't care how much you know until they know you care about them!"[5] In this book, we want to pull back the curtain and help you see life through your direct reports' eyes. Our goal is to increase your empathy or human-centric skill set and, in the process, help you develop skills and behaviors that allow you to lead at a higher level.

Insights

Your direct reports want you to . . .

- be true to your leadership style.
- model the desired behaviors you're looking to get from them.

CHAPTER 3

One Thing Every Bad Boss Lacks

I wish my manager would lead by example, manage with a soft touch, and quit being stupid and hypocritical.

*W*ould *you rather be a supervisor, manager, or leader?* Without fail, every time we ask that question to those present in the hundreds of leadership workshops we have delivered, the answer is always in unison: Be the leader! As Simon Sinek said, "I don't know what good leadership looks like, but I can tell you what bad leadership feels like."[1]

Before continuing, a few distinctions need to be made between these three roles. Here is the significant difference: While supervisors and managers are *appointed*, leaders *evolve*. Supervisors and managers tend to be rule enforcers, adhere to policies, and remain focused on day-to-day operations. Leaders are more often visionaries, inspirers, listeners, coaches, mentors, and supporters.

In the foreword for Simon Sinek's book *Leaders Eat Last*, retired general George Flynn wrote, "I know of no case study in history that describes an organization that has been managed out of a crisis. Every single one of them was led. Yet many of our educational institutions and training programs today are focused not on developing great leaders but on training effective managers."[2]

Flynn's words underscore the fundamental flaw in how we develop leaders and remind us of the importance of leadership. That said, to better understand how we shift from a supervisor or management mindset into becoming a high-performing leader, it is essential to understand some history of the evolution of management.

Three Management Styles

The classical style of management originated in the 1930s. This style originated from Fredrick Taylor and was called the *Scientific Style of Management* or the *Taylor Style of Management*. Based on this style, managers held all the reins of power, and workers operated at their mercy.[3] It represents the proper autocratic method, the *my way or the highway* mentality. When a problem occurred, the leader made all the decisions and then instructed workers on how to solve it.

We are reminded of a time when, delivering a team-building workshop at a manufacturing facility, no one sat on either side of the supervisor in the class. Typically, the workshop is high-energy with engaging activities and lively discussions. Oddly, this was not the case in this specific class. During the first break, three participants told me that the entire class would not speak openly with their supervisor present. For fear of retribution, they would remain silent.

The downside of this style was that collaboration was nonexistent. As a result, workers' motivation was low; they felt disempowered, lacked the desire to commit, and resorted to fulfilling their duties with mindless obedience. Let's also not forget the price companies paid as they were forced to live with decisions that only one person was making.

Realizing the classical style was often ineffective and only created more problems in the workplace, we moved to the opposite end of the spectrum in the early 1970s. Thinking that team meant being friends with our workers, a power shift was evident in the laissez-faire method, also known as the *Buddy–Buddy Style of Management*.[4] When a leader became aware of a problem, they turned decision-making over to workers to see the issue resolved. The challenge with this style is that chaos often ensued, and concerns were not effectively resolved. This style of management is a result of a leader who avoids conflict and wants to remain friends with everyone. Without clear expectations and willingness to manage team conflicts, failure is an expected consequence.

By the 1980s, we recognized some of the strengths and weaknesses each of these styles of management offered. By that point, there was a growing consensus that people should not be treated as cogs in a wheel, and a team approach was needed. To be effective, a merger of the two styles was required. Strong leaders were needed, but they could not operate like dictators and had to listen to the advice of those on their team. With this in mind, companies began to scale down their workforce to become leaner. Gone were the days when paying a hundred employees and only twenty-five doing the deep thinking was acceptable. Everyone on the team needed to participate.

An example that comes to mind is when a leader who graduated from our Emerging Leader program soon faced a significant challenge. A malfunctioning engine needed to be fixed in time for the next race. The engine arrived at the facility in early December, two and a half weeks before the company's holiday shutdown. Knowing this could disrupt people's holiday plans and knowing he did not want to make arbitrary decisions telling the team how to resolve the challenge, he collaborated with the team. Together, they strategically planned and completed the project before the holiday break. Collaboration indeed leads to stronger commitments.

From this philosophy came the concept of *human-centric leadership*. When leaders become aware of a problem today, they collaborate with their teammates (direct reports) and solve problems together.

This human-centric approach to leadership continues to be effective because there is more diversity and critical thinking, people are empowered, and more productivity occurs. The downside is that it can take a long time. Unfortunately, many leaders are not trained this way, and companies often default to the antiquated autocratic approach, producing short-term results but impacting long-term dissension and turnover.

Human-Centric Leadership

The main goal of human-centric leadership is to shift the focus and help leaders become more people-focused. The effectiveness of human-centric leadership is tied to the root of human behavior. Every person needs to feel autonomous, that their opinions matter, and that they are valuable. Direct reports want to have a voice or at least input when a decision is made, and when they do not, it can directly impact their engagement and morale. They need to feel like they belong and want to feel included. Do not underestimate the value of asking direct reports for their ideas because it creates engagement.

We created a list of human behavior *truisms* that apply to all direct reports. Therefore, it would be helpful if all leaders understood and applied the truisms in their role:

- **Direct reports need to feel autonomous.**

  » **Leaders Application**: Engage direct reports and inquire about their thoughts and feelings. Ask for their opinions and create a psychologically safe environment free of retribution.

- **Direct reports are curious and need to be challenged.**

  » **Leaders Application**: Boredom and monotony cannibalize motivation and passion. Create stretch goals and cross-train direct reports as much as possible.

- **Direct reports who are intrinsically driven are more committed and motivated than extrinsically driven people.**

  » **Leaders Application**: Intrinsic motivation is what inspires people. Place less emphasis on extrinsic rewards and more on the things individuals deem inherently important.

- **Direct reports are different and should be treated as individuals.**

  » **Leaders Application**: Although direct reports may walk to a different beat, they may have the best idea. Leverage each person's uniqueness.

- **Direct reports are likely to live up to the trust that is given to them.**

  » **Leaders Application**: If you want your direct reports to trust you, show them you trust them.

- **Direct reports learn to make decisions by making decisions.**

  » **Leaders Application**: If you make all the decisions, you are blinded from seeing other possibilities. Collaborating with your direct reports to make decisions allows for better decisions and enhances the person's level of empowerment.

I Didn't Realize Leadership Was Like This!

Several years ago, one of the participants who graduated from our leadership academy sent us an email sharing her perspective one month after receiving a promotion. She mentioned several things she did not understand when she first became a leader. Some examples include not realizing how quickly she defaulted to being a micromanager. In addition, she did not understand how important it was to develop people, even when she was consumed with other management responsibilities. As she transitioned into her leadership role, it became clear that her teammates knew she had their backs.

She went on to share how she had no idea what problem-solving looked like as a leader. Her team would often come to her to *solve a problem*. If she didn't know the answer, she felt inadequate. She didn't realize that as a leader, problem-solving could be collaborative among her team and that she didn't always need to have the answer.

As she admitted, it is too easy for her to revert to her former style of being a doer instead of leading a team. Adding to this is the stress of leading her former teammates and peers. She now recognizes she was blinded by not realizing she was responsible not only for herself but for her entire team. She now understands what it's like to be an insightful leader.

After reading this email, we smiled because we could see this new leader got it.

Six Styles of Leadership

Following a three-year study of three thousand middle managers, best-selling author Daniel Goleman found that most leaders utilize six distinct leadership styles: authoritative, coaching, affiliate, democratic, pacesetter, and coercive. Leaders with the best results relied on more than one style of management. They viewed them as clubs in their golf bags, pulling out different styles as situations changed.[5]

First was the *authoritative* style. Leaders who gravitate toward this style are visionaries motivated by linking work to the organization's vision. They allow people to innovate, experiment, and take calculated risks.

Second was the *coaching* style. The focus here was on developing people for the future, identifying strengths and weaknesses, and being good at delegation.

Then there is the *affiliate* style of leadership, which appeared most effective when operating in conjunction with an authoritative leadership style. Leaders who implemented this style generally valued individuals, created harmony, and were masters at creating a sense of belonging among their teams.

The fourth is the *democratic* style. This represents leaders who shined when a difficult decision needed to be made. They built consensus through participation and being great listeners. Goleman noticed that this style drove flexibility, responsibility, and commitment.

The fifth style is the *pacesetter*. According to Goleman, leaders who utilize the pacesetting style should use it sparingly. Pacesetters are obsessed with excellence and doing things better and faster. They identify poor performance, and if there is no improvement, they will quickly make a change. The downside is that this fast-paced leadership style can breed distrust and burnout.

The sixth and final style is what Goleman termed *coercive* leadership. This is the least practical approach, focusing on top-down decision-making. It demands immediate compliance, leading to a disempowered team.

What Most Leaders Lack

Most leaders gravitate toward one or two leadership styles. Most effective leaders tend to use all their leadership style golf clubs; unfortunately, many leaders remain blinded or lack the self-awareness to utilize their different clubs. As in the game of golf, how would you expect to hit a nice chip shot fifty yards from the putting green if the only club you have in your bag is a driver? Each situation a leader encounters requires a different approach. Leadership is situational, just like the game of golf.

Insightful leaders recognize two bedrock principles of leadership. The first is that leaders lead people, not widgets. Second, every person is a social creature and has social needs. John Maxwell stated this perfectly in *21 Irrefutable Laws of Leadership*, "You can't move people to action unless you first move them with emotions. The heart comes before the head."[6]

Neuroscience has affirmed the works of Salovey, Mayer, Goleman, and others regarding people's needs in the workplace. For example, social and emotional needs like feeling appreciated and respected activate the brain's reward system, just like a financial bonus does.[7] It is incumbent upon leaders to recognize and address these social-emotional needs within all their organization's direct reports.

As HR professionals, we have seen the following scenario play out countless times. An organization reaches out, and the script goes like this: We have a problem! Last year, we hired Sal to fill this new role in our organization. His technical understanding is exceptional, and we do not want to let him go. But our problem is that he cannot get along with anyone in our organization! He is abrasive, lacks a filter, is poor at communicating, has zero empathy, and is demanding. What should we do?

Each time we hear this script play out, we think, here is a person who has risen to a position of power because they are technically capable or able to drive results at any cost, but they lack that which is most important: social-emotional intelligence. Author Malcolm

Gladwell writes, "We have a sense of what a leader is supposed to look like, and that stereotype is so powerful that when someone fits it, we simply become blind to other considerations."[8] Ultimately, this lack of social-emotional understanding significantly damages this person's career, those they lead, and their entire organization.

Leadership Styles Are Timeless

Different leadership styles will always exist. New trends and fads will come and go as the years progress, but the need for leaders who possess a human-centric skill set will last forever.

Because leadership is all about relationships and influence, your partnerships with your direct reports, peers, bosses, and customers are critical. Every leader must learn to adapt to the situations they face. They must adjust their approach, style, and behaviors to meet the needs of others. The foundation of leadership is not theory. It's not about keeping up with today's latest philosophies, terms, jargon, traits, and styles. Insightful leadership is about applying the skills and behaviors you have developed.

The common need for human-centric leadership will remain through the changing winds of time. Being a respectful listener, receiving feedback, asking questions, building trust, coaching others to succeed, and having difficult conversations are all qualities that will never go out of style! With this in mind and years of training and coaching leaders, we created the ten commandments of an insightful leader.

Ten Commandments of Insightful Leaders

1. They modify their old, antiquated behavior and thinking habits.

2. They influence and persuade people in nonmanipulative ways.

3. They invite healthy debate and never fight to be right.

4. They never throw the company under the bus despite disapproval and change.

5. They remain calm and assertive when reinforcing limits and dealing with negative behavior.

6. They recognize and manage their implicit biases.

7. They demonstrate empathic communication and address nonverbal communication.

8. They are strategic and thoughtful in times of change.

9. They are role models who always act ethically and with integrity.

10. They maintain optimism, recognizing that feelings are contagious.

Insights

Your direct reports want you to . . .

- use different approaches to leadership.

- model the desired behaviors you're looking to get from your direct reports.

.

CHAPTER 4

Neuroscience and Leadership

It's so frustrating when my manager flip-flops from one decision to another. It's as if my manager has two different brains.

Throughout this book, many chapters discuss neuroscience's insights on the topics covered. Neuroscience studies how our anatomy, physiology, biochemistry, and nervous system affect our thoughts, feelings, and behavior. As a result, skills that organizations once considered *soft skills* for leaders to possess are now seen as essential *hard skills*.

Ponder this quote, as we will revisit it at the end of the chapter. "Imagine if you could proactively guide your neural activity along pathways that made you naturally more able to ignore distractions and inference (the infernal email alerts), regulate emotional responses to achieve your desired behaviors, solve problems, and integrate 'data' from the external environment and your inner world to reach goals. Interestingly, this is the goal of all good organizations [and leaders]."[1]

Leadership has been studied extensively since the Industrial Revolution but remains somewhat confusing. Are leaders born with specific traits, or does a particular personality style drive them to lead? What distinguishes an exceptional leader from an average one? Despite numerous theories and catchy leadership titles, the deeper dynamics that make a leader truly effective remain elusive.

However, neuroscience has clarified these questions and provides scientific insights into how the brain functions in various areas, including leadership. Some of these areas include decision-making, emotional management, civility and respect, social-emotional intelligence, and rewiring the brain.

Decision-Making

It's been discovered that 46 percent of companies that go bankrupt do so because of poor decision-making by their leaders.[2] This means that decision-making is a critical skill for leaders and for the success of the company they work for.

Neuroscience has revealed, for example, that cognitive biases are responsible for poor decision-making and are a critical blind spot for most people. Everyone has cognitive biases because it's a natural function of the brain. We make decisions based on our life experiences and thinking habits.

For example, you probably watch CNN if you're a Democrat or Fox News if you are a Republican (confirmation bias). When a leader is quick to blame others after a mistake is made, that's self-serving bias. Since the brain is designed to create biases, it is critically important to recognize that our biases can lend themselves to positive or negative outcomes. Recognizing this reality will help you make the best decision, though not always the easiest.

Since the brain is always looking for shortcuts, it will gravitate toward what it already knows or has done in the past. But often this information is incorrect and leads us down the wrong path. This is why leaders should avoid making quick, emotional decisions.

Emotional Management

Are you struggling with managing stress and emotions as a leader? As many of us have experienced, it's essential to understand how your emotional state can impact those around you. As neuroscientists continue to study the contagious nature of emotions, they have discovered mirror neurons in the brain that activate when observing similar behavior in others. For instance, if you see someone yawn, you'll often yawn. Similarly, watching a sad movie can make you feel down. That said, consider how your mood and feelings affect your direct reports, peers, clients, etc. Failing to regulate your emotions may have many unintended consequences for you, your team, your decision-making, and the organization.

The good news is that you can improve your emotional regulation skills. Dr. Matthew Lieberman from the UCLA Department of Psychology discovered that the brain has a *braking system* that can control many impulses, which can be strengthened with practice.[3] In the course on Social and Emotional Intelligence, which we teach as part of our corporate leadership curriculum, we show leaders the adverse effects of suppressing emotions and provide them with a straightforward method of labeling their feelings—a good way to strengthen the braking system. This task is difficult, however, especially since many leaders believe there is no place for emotions in the workplace. That belief is what we consider a significant leadership blind spot.

Civility and Respect

As humans, we are continually dealing with various social issues. These issues can range from being excluded or hurt due to our different beliefs to facing ridicule from negative individuals (leaders) who project their feelings onto others. The psychological pain people feel is real and cannot be easily dismissed. Or have you ever given negative feedback to a direct report during a performance review, and they became defensive? This is a natural response because a specific part of the brain perceives the feedback as a physical attack, which can make the person defensive. You might be confused about why they reacted that way, but it all comes down to brain chemistry.

The work of Naomi Eisenberger, for example, treats social pain much like physical pain.[4] She found that "feeling socially excluded activates some of the same neural regions that are activated in response to physical pain, suggesting that social rejection may indeed be painful."[5] In another study, scientists successfully used Tylenol to reduce social pain.[6] In Chapter 19 we will discuss the importance of creating a psychologically safe work culture.

The Brain

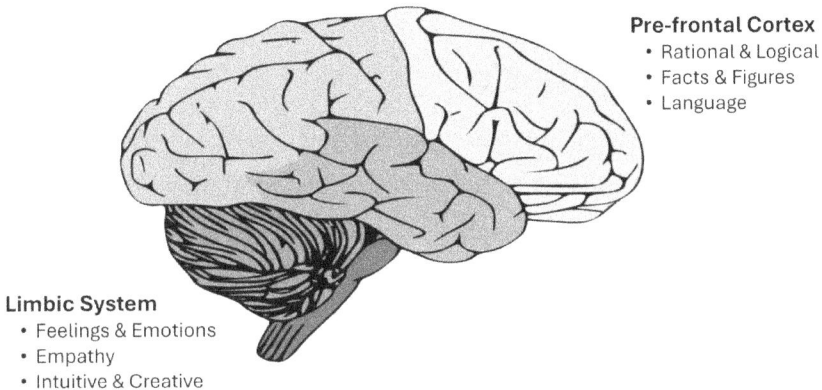

Pre-frontal Cortex
- Rational & Logical
- Facts & Figures
- Language

Limbic System
- Feelings & Emotions
- Empathy
- Intuitive & Creative

Social-Emotional Intelligence

Although we dedicate Chapter 5 to social-emotional intelligence (SEI), we want to clarify the brain science associated with SEI in this chapter. In 2012, a study by Richard E. Boyatzis and his colleagues at Case Western Reserve University showed that leaders with a resonant leadership style, specifically ones with high levels of empathy and emotional intelligence, are more effective than dissonant leaders who use a coercive and authoritarian style.[7] They found that employees whose leaders used a resonant style were more socially aware, attentive, and able to establish more positive relationships.

In contrast, leaders utilizing a dissonant style activated negative emotions in their employees, as well as a decrease in social awareness and limited attention. Furthermore, research has shown that leaders who use more social language are perceived by their direct reports as more motivating and engaging, elements of a socially and emotionally intelligent person.[8]

Rewiring the Brain

The field of neuroscience has made exciting discoveries about neuroplasticity. Previously, it was believed that the brain only changed and developed during childhood. However, research has revealed that neuroplasticity persists throughout adulthood. This means that the brain remains adaptable and capable of learning and adjusting to new situations throughout life.

We now know that people can actively *rewire* their brains, which was previously considered impossible. For instance, individuals who repeatedly use self-affirmation can alter their thinking patterns to feel better about themselves. As leadership coaches, we often assist leaders in modifying their thoughts and behaviors. This can involve changing one's mindset from "Direct reports get paid to do their jobs; I don't need to constantly praise them," to "It's important to provide positive feedback to my team to boost morale and productivity." Or from this, "I need to closely supervise my team to get work done around here," to "I need to demonstrate trustworthy behaviors to build more trust with my direct reports and trust my team's abilities." The evidence is clear: Providing positive feedback leads to and sustains behavioral change.

A 2006 article by David Rock and Jeffrey Schwartz, *Neuroscience in Leadership: Breakthroughs in Brain Research Explain How to Make Organizational Transformation Succeed*, discusses organizational change and how the following bullet points would not have been accepted several years ago:[9]

- Change creates discomfort for many reasons. Besides losses associated with change, it can create physical pain.

- Rewards and punishment can influence behavioral change temporarily, but changing one's thinking is the key to long-term success.

- Verbal persuasion is the weakest form of influencing behavioral change.

- Focus your attention and the malleable brain can reshape itself.

- Perception becomes your reality.

Neuroscience has brought a greater understanding of the interplay of thoughts, feelings, and behavior. Every interaction a leader has in the workplace affects everyone with whom they come into contact. From a morning hello to a performance coaching meeting, our body and brain consistently emit messages to people around us.[10] These powerful messages can easily connect or disconnect us from one another.

In summary, let's revisit Swart's quotation found at the beginning of the chapter:

"Imagine if you could proactively guide your neural activity along pathways that made you naturally more able to ignore distractions and inference (the infernal email alerts), regulate emotional responses to achieve your desired behaviors, solve problems, and integrate 'data' from the external environment and your inner world to reach goals."[11]

Imagine how effective you can be as a leader by doing what Swart asked. As you gain insight into what your direct reports expect and want from their leaders, keep an open mind and consider how this new scientific knowledge can improve your leadership skills and abilities.

Insights

Your direct reports want you to . . .

- keep an open mind and apply the updated neuroscience.
- rewire old thinking and communication habits.

SKILLS OF A LEADER

CHAPTER 5

Social and Emotional Intelligence

It would be nice if she could be less egocentric,
increase her emotional intelligence, and
connect with everyone on the team.

Who is the best leader you have ever reported to, and what made them great? This is a question we ask participants in our course on social-emotional intelligence. No matter who is in attendance, the responses are always the same. People from different backgrounds and industries agree that they respect compassionate, motivating, positive, caring, and authentic leaders. In other words, they appreciate and value social characteristics. Rarely, if ever, do we hear terms like *brilliant, technically sound*, or *intelligent* because we have discovered that one's social-emotional intelligence acts like a magnet to attract and connect a leader to their direct reports.

A leader's day consists of ongoing interactions with the people who interact with them. From conversations in the break room about the news, sports, and weather to critical discussions, we use our social and emotional intelligence. Social and emotional intelligence combined enhances a leader's effectiveness by being more self-aware and socially aware. It helps them manage their emotions and build lasting relationships. Combine this with sound technical understanding, and you have a leader on the fast track to true success.

As we coach and develop leaders, we often encounter individuals stuck in place and seemingly unable to advance in their careers. They are puzzled and cannot figure out the reasons why. In many respects, they are great at what they do and often explain how they took several leadership classes. "I could write a book about leadership skills," one leader explained. And he was probably correct! The truth is that most leaders know a lot about the skills needed to be successful. However, there is a missing ingredient and critical error in their thinking. Like most skill sets, leadership requires more than an intellectual and theoretical understanding; it demands practical application and execution. These well-intended leaders lack the magic sauce of social-emotional intelligence.

Social and emotional intelligence has been studied and researched for decades. The relationship of SEI is correlated to a leader's success, income, health, and overall life satisfaction. Ultimately, it boils down to the people management skills that propel a leader's career.[1]

What Is Social-Emotional Intelligence?

Social intelligence is a subset of emotional intelligence. It is the ability to use emotional intelligence in social situations. It is being able to recognize the needs of others and to connect with people in a socially acceptable manner.

All of this recalls a personal illustration. Keith's friend, Doug, is one of the most intelligent people I know. One day, while having dinner at his home, we turned on the TV show *Jeopardy!* I was amazed at how quickly he answered the questions before the contestants could push their buttons. He was dialed in, answering almost every question with pinpoint accuracy. I firmly believe he would have won thousands of dollars if he were a contestant. With a seemingly photographic memory, he is beyond the traditional definition of intelligence.

But there is another side to Doug—his social side, or lack thereof. Doug lives as a hermit in a home by himself. He graduated from engineering school and worked for several years, hating every minute of it. He played the stock market well and eventually stopped working at age forty-five. His days consist of exercising, reading, and watching the news. He has no commitments, few hobbies, limited social interaction, and is not comfortable interacting with people. Even as I tell this story, I shake my head, thinking how a person with such a brilliant mind can be socially inept.

Here is the point. There are many Dougs in leadership positions in the workplace. They are great doers but have trouble getting along with people. Behind the scenes, their direct reports are saying things like, "I wish they had even an ounce of empathy," "If only they were more involved," or "They are so insecure and self-centered!"

To clarify, SEI is not to be confused with being too soft of a leader or becoming best friends with those who report to you. A leader with high social-emotional intelligence blends their technical skills and knowledge with human skills that enable them to connect with people intellectually and emotionally.

Many organizations have too many of the TV character Mr. Spock from the television series *Star Trek* in leadership positions. In *Star Trek*, Mr. Spock is a Vulcan. On the show, the species of Vulcans lack emotions, as they are all logical compared to humans.[2] There is an obvious cost to organizations with leaders who lack SEI; leaders with a strong SEI reap the benefits.

Consider the following:

- The higher a leader's emotional intelligence, the better the climate in the workplace.[3]

- Leaders with high emotional intelligence make $29,000 more annually than leaders with low emotional intelligence.[4]

- Emotional intelligence has a positive correlation with performance, which indicates that it is a significant predictor of job performance.[5]

- Executives with higher levels of empathy, self-regard, reality testing, and problem-solving were more likely to yield high profit-earning companies.[6]

- Leaders with high emotional intelligence were likelier to succeed than those with a high IQ or substantial work experience.[7]

Four Quadrants of SEI

There are four quadrants of a social-emotional intelligence model that is greatly influenced by Daniel Goleman's research. The upper quadrants of the model contain the emotionally intelligent side, and the lower two quadrants address the socially intelligent side of people.

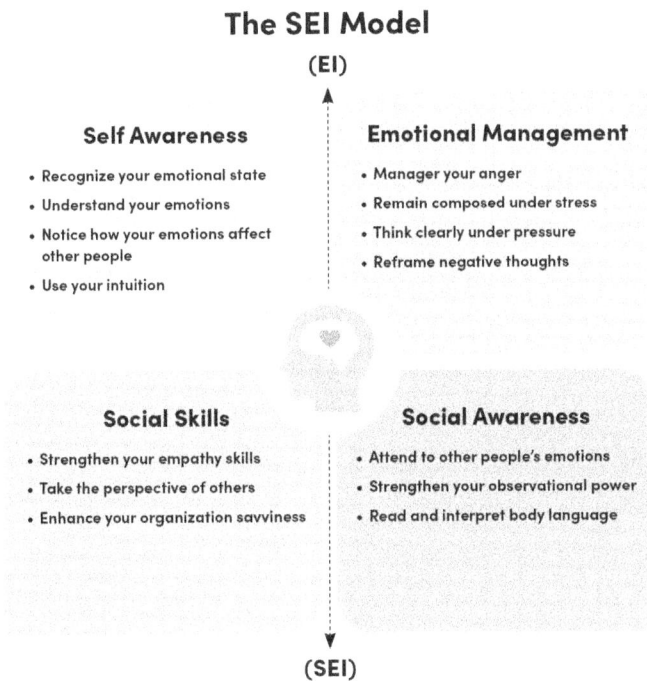

The SEI Model

(EI)

Self Awareness
- Recognize your emotional state
- Understand your emotions
- Notice how your emotions affect other people
- Use your intuition

Emotional Management
- Manager your anger
- Remain composed under stress
- Think clearly under pressure
- Reframe negative thoughts

Social Skills
- Strengthen your empathy skills
- Take the perspective of others
- Enhance your organization savviness

Social Awareness
- Attend to other people's emotions
- Strengthen your observational power
- Read and interpret body language

(SEI)

Self-Awareness

All behavior changes begin with self-awareness. It is difficult to change something you're unaware of. It is critically important for leaders to see the connection between how they view themselves and how others perceive them. Doing so influences your ability to lead, be successful, and develop impactful work and personal relationships. Self-awareness is the starting point for self-improvement and social and emotional intelligence.

Think about some of our favorite TV shows with characters who lack self-awareness. What comes to mind? Television show characters such as Sheldon from *The Big Bang Theory*, Steve Urkel from *Family Matters*, Michael Scott from *The Office*, and George Constanza and Elaine Benes from *Seinfeld*. Now, think about the people you work with or have worked with. What is it like to work with them?

Recognize and pay attention to your internal body sensations, body language, thoughts, feelings, and behavior to enhance your self-awareness. Additionally, learn to trust the intuitive moments and those *gut feelings*. Albert Einstein once said, "The intellect has little to do on the road to discovery. There comes a leap in consciousness, call it intuition or what you will, when the solution comes to you, and you don't know how or why."[8]

Finally, since neuroscience has taught us that feelings are contagious, be mindful about how you want to feel and how you want the people around you to feel. Be self-aware.

Emotional Management

Picture yourself in the operating room about to go under for a surgical procedure. As you wait to be induced by the anesthesiologist, you notice the primary surgeon and a nurse bickering back and forth. As the voices intensify with anger, you see the surgeon rip the phone out of the wall and throw it at the nurse! Fortunately for her, his aim was poor. You have someone who appears technically competent but, as Goleman states, is an emotional hijack.[9]

Unfortunately, situations like this happen in the workplace far too often. Maybe not to the extent as seen in the previous example, but we can all relate to acts of unprofessional behavior at some point in our career. When stress levels increase, so do our emotional levels. Emotions play a critical part in your everyday behavior and relationships, and learning to control your emotions can be the difference between establishing and maintaining successful relationships.

Emotions are determined by the way we think about a particular situation. Changing your thoughts about the situation can change or modify your feelings and behaviors. For example, you were transferred to a new division within your company. While this new role has increased the length of your daily commute, it may have also allowed you to connect more often with friends and family by calling them on your cell phone during your daily drive. As we will further explore in Chapter 8, our ability to reframe our *stinking thinking* is the most effective way to keep our emotions in check.

Social Awareness

An excellent example of the lack of social awareness is the movie *Groundhog Day* with Bill Murray. In this classic comedy film, Bill Murray plays a character named Phil Connors, a television weatherman. There is a scene in which he is confronted by a guy named Ned, a former classmate from school. Phil, unable to recognize Ned, continues to walk along. Ned doesn't realize Phil's obvious negative body language, which is screaming out, "Leave me alone!" Instead, Ned continues to walk alongside Phil, trying to trigger the teenage recollection from high school and then also trying to sell him life insurance. Finally, after a brief conversation, Ned asks Phil what he is doing for dinner. Phil's response, "Something else!"[10]

It does not require a profound psychological interpretation to discern the negative messages Phil was sending to Ned, and it is what makes this comedic scene so hilarious. The problem is that there can be several characters like Ned who seem to pop up in our everyday workplace. They are oblivious to the micro messages others send and can be found in the office with unwelcome interruptions, interjections into a private conversation between two colleagues, and other rude or oblivious conduct. However, remember that we all have various tolerance levels for social interaction.

While you may not necessarily want to rehash the latest ball game with one of your direct reports leaning on the office door while trying to remain focused in front of your computer, it's essential to find balance. To avoid becoming another Ned, you must strengthen your observational power. This is essential in connecting with your direct reports and increasing social and emotional intelligence.

It never ceases to amaze me when I go to the grocery store and walk to the checkout with only one item, only to end up waiting in line behind another person who has fifty items in their cart. Someone with heightened social awareness would say, "You have one item. Please, go ahead!" But the lack of being socially aware ignores the obvious and makes people like me wait their turn. People are often so myopic in their thinking that they fail to notice their surroundings. For a leader, this type of blindness will limit their ability to establish positive relationships in their workplace.

Observing your direct report's body movements, facial expressions, posture, and energy levels while interacting with them is crucial to maximizing your connection. You may want to share some of these observations with your direct reports when appropriate. For example, you communicated some information in a meeting with a person and observed that they rolled their eyes. You may say, "I see that you rolled your eyes. It appears you disagree with what I said." At this point, you are now opening the door to a further connection with the person, as opposed to either not being aware of their behavior or, even worse, choosing to passively dismiss or avoid what you observed.

Social Skills

Earlier, we asked you to think about the best leader you have ever had. Again, almost all participants in our training describe the social skills—rather than the technical skills—of their best boss. We hear words like caring, motivational, supportive, appreciative, and so forth.

Now, we have another question for you to consider. Identify a person in your life you find to be extraordinary, someone who made an impact in your life. What is remarkable about them? A similar list probably comes to mind when asked about an impactful leader. People are attracted to those with excellent social and emotional skills. There is a plethora of social skills for leaders to embrace. Many of these skills, including empathy, motivation, and perspective-taking, will be further addressed in upcoming chapters. However, there are a few additional ones that are important to explore.

Your Leadership Brand

Have you ever wondered what comes to mind for your leaders, colleagues, customers, or, most importantly, direct reports when your name is mentioned? Every leader, manager, employee, at every level, has a personal brand—a reputation. Your brand impacts your ability to achieve results that can either fuel or derail your long-term career goals. Like a product brand, your brand consists of complex characteristics and dynamics that play out daily. What you say or don't say affects your brand. What you stand for and choose to ignore will add to your brand. Your brand is who you are! Think of your leadership brand as a "mosaic, made up of many different impressions that combine to form a picture of you in someone else's mind."[11] It's your reputation and how you are perceived and experienced in the workplace.

Knowing your leadership brand allows you to see the blind spots (pitfalls) other leaders would miss when engaging with people. Through a more consistent leadership brand, you should be able to:

- communicate clearly to others how you add value,
- have consistency and focus on the message you send to others,
- have increased efficiency in how you spend your time,
- have confidence in your personal skills, and
- grow your career.

Personal Accountability

Thirty-eight percent of our survey respondents said they would fire their boss because their boss did not accept accountability for their own behavior. We heard things like: "I wish he would stop pointing fingers and just look in the mirror!"

Personal accountability is taking responsibility for your thoughts, feelings, and behaviors. It is easy to understand but not so easy to practice. What has become the norm for many in our society is to blame our misfortunes on others. "It's because my parent didn't give me X." "If the engineering department had done X, then we wouldn't have this problem." "It's not my fault; I gave it to X." Maybe these and other comments prompted the great scientist George Washington Carver to state, "Ninety-nine percent of all failures come from people who have a habit of making excuses."[12]

Personal accountability begins with taking responsibility for your actions and having the emotional courage to admit your mistakes and lack of knowledge. In our attempt to protect our ego and self-esteem, we often shift blame onto others. Being vulnerable in our thinking, feelings, and behavior is risky, and it can be challenging for leaders to stand alone. As researcher Peter Bregman notes: "Emotional courage means standing apart from others without separating yourself from them. It means speaking up when others are silent. And remaining steadfast, grounded, and measured in the face of uncertainty."[13]

Admitting you don't know something or admitting your mistakes are not signs of weakness. Instead, they demonstrate your integrity and willingness to be open-minded, which increases trustworthiness. Steve Young, the great retired quarterback from the San Francisco 49ers, gave an eloquent speech about leadership and accountability. He explained how he threw 202 interceptions in his career. When asked why it happened, he initially blamed the sun, the wet ball, a blown route, and other mitigating circumstances. But by doing so, it demotivated his teammates, which weakened his position as a leader in their eyes.

As he matured, he recognized the importance of personal accountability, and instead of listing the whys, he began to own it and began making statements like: "I screwed up. Here is what we are going to do to win the game." This created positive energy among his teammates and led them to become more accountable for their behavior. Young said it perfectly: "People will respond when you (the leader) demonstrate personal accountability."[14]

Remember this simple mantra: You cannot go wrong when you see it, own it, solve it, and do it.[15]

Insights

Your direct reports want you to . . .

- effectively manage your emotions to build lasting relationships.

- demonstrate personal accountability and take responsibility for your actions.

- show emotional courage and admit your own mistakes or lack of knowledge.

CHAPTER 6

Communicate Like an Adult

I hate it when he speaks to me in
a condescending manner.

Several weeks into writing this book, Keith spent the holidays with his daughter's family in Chicago. That evening, he helped her prepare a meal of fresh swordfish and Dungeness crab. As they worked together to prepare the meal, his daughter asked him to place the crackers on the dining room table. This struck him as an odd request, but he obliged and scanned the nearby counter but couldn't find any crackers.

"Where are they?" Keith asked.

"On the table behind you," she replied.

Turning around, Keith saw nothing and grew agitated. "Where? I don't see a box of crackers!"

Immediately, his daughter and son-in-law broke out in laughter. Their reference to crackers was the utensils used to *crack* open crabs.

This short interaction made Keith chuckle and reminded him how easily misunderstandings can occur in the most basic communications.

Communication Is More than an Art

Until recently, communication had always been considered an art form. However, recent neuroscience breakthroughs have revealed that communication is no longer a soft skill, which corporate trainers and organizational psychologists have intuitively known for years. Neuroscience provides a valuable understanding of how the brain processes information and how we communicate this information.

Communication is more than an art. It is a necessity—a primary function of human behavior. However, communication has changed significantly as society has evolved into the information age. The use of texts, emails, and other technology doesn't meet the need for genuinely advanced communication. From personal relationships at home to how direct reports communicate in the workplace, these new tools and methods have led us to connect differently with one another. Communication challenges are everywhere, and as a psychologist, this is perhaps the most significant challenge Keith deals with in his private practice. When Mrs. and Mr. Smith walk into his office for counseling, and he asks them what brings them in, more often than not, the first words out of their mouths are, "We can't communicate!"

Think of the global challenges many countries face today, such as the threat of war or domestic political issues. Underlying much of this breakdown is not only a difference in ideology but a breakdown in the ability to have rational conversations with people who hold disagreements.

Let's not forget the workplace, a breeding ground for communication challenges. And as one engineer barked out in one of our workshops, "This communication stuff is complicated!" Workplace communication is integral to team effectiveness and impacts the organization's bottom line. If you desire to advance in your career continually and successfully, keep in mind that approximately 94 percent of people agree that a person with excellent communication skills is more likely to be promoted than people with a high level of technical competencies but weak communication skills.[1]

What Makes Effective Communication So Difficult?

Thus far, we have described how communication plays a critical role in everyone's personal and professional lives. Yet, all of us struggle in this area. Think of the numerous books, workshops, seminars, and articles on communication. Ask yourself what blockers get in the way of your ability to communicate effectively.

Your list would likely mirror the list that leaders capture in our workshop:

- Personalities
- Lack of time or skill
- Poor listening

- Ego

- Different agendas

- Emotions

These are just six of the countless number of communication blockers. Considering the number of factors standing in your way of communicating effectively, can you better understand the struggle? Regardless of your position in the organization, your intelligence, and even your desire to communicate perfectly, it's challenging to do so consistently.

Even as professionals in leadership development, we will be the first to admit that we struggle to consistently communicate at a high level. Sometimes we get distracted, or our mind wanders when we need to be focused on the person in front of us. In fact, if you witnessed some of the arguments because of ineffective communication we had in writing this book, you might say to yourself, "I wouldn't buy their book!"

The following story from Keith underscores the preceding points. It was October 19, 1987, and I had just stepped out of my office to greet my 4:00 p.m. patient sitting in the waiting room. As is often the case, the news channel playing in the waiting room was on that day, and I could not help but overhear the dismal report. As I greeted my patient, the local news anchor shared some of the stunning details of a dark day in the stock market that has since been called Black Monday. On that day, the stock market tanked and fell more than 20 percent in only a few short hours—one of the largest stock market plunges in a single day. As luck would have it, I had purchased stock the previous Friday!

Immediately, my mind could not help but drift. Almost instantly, my focus for that session was replaced with negative thoughts that swirled around in my mind. "I'm going to lose everything. Will I even be able to pay the mortgage?" My mind was everywhere but where it needed to be, which was on my patient.

Driving home that night, I felt a twinge of remorse. I thought about how I had not been present during that session, as my mind was flooded with anxious thoughts. Even if the patient hadn't noticed, I made a mental note not to charge him for the session. When he returned the following Monday for his next appointment, I told him the truth about my unfortunate luck the previous week and the impact I believe it had on my ability to remain focused during our session. I shared with him my intent not to charge him for that session. He looked at me and said, "I assumed something was wrong. I thought you were sick or something." I smiled at him and responded, "You have no idea how sick I was!"

The point of this story is significant. I was the *professional*, and as much as I tried to hide my feelings, my patient knew! As I experienced that day, there are many times our preoccupation with current events causes us to half-listen to people, leading to a disconnection. But when this happens, it is essential to be accountable. This is the time to look directly at the person and say something like, "I'm sorry my mind wandered for a moment. Can you please repeat that?" Remember, they already know you were half-listening. When you own it, you regain credibility.

As Sigmund Freud noted, "Our bodies are always talking." In every interaction, we constantly display micro behaviors to one another. These micro behaviors happen in a split second, often received at an unconscious level by the speaker. It is estimated that people express two thousand to four thousand micro behaviors per day.[2] These messages can either hurt or enhance the very essence of the relationship at that moment.

Consider this simple example: While conversing with someone, you glance at your phone. In that moment, you just sent a micro message. On an unconscious level, the person interacting with you might interpret this micro behavior as though you lost interest or that you do not care to listen to what they have to say.

As seen by the preceding stories and experiences, communication can be challenging. Between the numerous communication blockers and micro behaviors, leaders often experience a disconnection with their direct reports. William Hollingsworth (though it is often attributed to George Bernard Shaw) expressed it eloquently when he said, "The single biggest problem in communication is the illusion that it has taken place."[3]

Four Styles of Communication

Your personality, how your brain is wired, and your childhood experiences contribute to how you communicate. People tend to gravitate to four primary communication styles: passive, passive-aggressive, aggressive, and assertive. As we explore each of these styles further, try to uncover which communication styles you are most likely to use.

PASSIVE

Passive communicators tend to be more submissive when communicating. This leader speaks softly and has trouble voicing their true feelings. Passive communicators in the workplace will chronically agree (they avoid conflict) and sit on the fence when a decision needs to be made.

PASSIVE-AGGRESSIVE

The passive-aggressive leader appears innocent and passive when communicating. However, below the passivity lies anger that plays out indirectly. This indirect anger manifests in sarcasm, complaining, and placing blame on others through gossip channels. This could be seen in the workplace through compliments delivered backhandedly, leaving you uncertain if you have just been praised or insulted. For example, "You did an amazing job on that project . . . for someone with your skill set."

AGGRESSIVE

The aggressive leader is the opposite of the passive approach and focuses on being as direct as possible. Leaders who use this form of interaction believe the best defense is a strong offense. Aggressive leaders often speak loudly and firmly, which may intimidate those around them. They appear so sure of themselves that the door of communication is slammed shut by those who oppose their views. In the workplace, these highly visible leaders are the ones direct reports tend to avoid for fear of getting caught in the crossfire.

ASSERTIVE

An assertive leader leads by often expressing their thoughts, ideas, and expectations in a self-assured but considerate way. Assertive leadership also involves collaboration with people at all levels of an organization. Leaders who use an assertive style when communicating have found an effective midpoint between not being too aggressive or too passive. It's become clear to us this is the most effective style of communication because assertive leaders can achieve goals without destroying others' self-esteem and it allows them to treat everyone with respect and dignity. In the workplace, these leaders are the ones who tend to ask instead of tell, and they engage and collaborate often.

Communicate Like an Adult

During our years of coaching and training leaders, we have found that one model stands out as the most effective. It is a simple and easily understood model that can be put into practice immediately. Whenever we reconnect with people who have attended our workshops, they often share stories of how this model helped them succeed in their careers.

The theory was first presented in Dr. Thomas Harris's 1967 self-help book, *I'm OK, You're OK: A Practical Guide to Transactional Analysis*.[4] In it, Harris highlights a contrast between three ego states—Child, Parent, and Adult (here we've changed the terms to *states of mind*). These three states exist in all people.

THE CHILD

The *child state of mind* contains the creative, fun-loving part of who we are. Examples are found when we play sports or allow ourselves the freedom to be a little silly, such as innocently picking up a snowball on a wintery afternoon and tossing it at a coworker when walking to the parking lot. However, there exists a flipside with the *child* and the *parent* states of mind. This is seen when a person yells and spews insults or exclaims an excuse like, "This is not my job . . . !"

THE PARENT

As we grow older, we integrate and develop the *parent state of mind.* This state consists of the beliefs and attitudes learned from authority figures. Parents, teachers, clergy, and other adult figures contribute to this mindset. This state of mind involves taking on more responsibility and following the laws of society and the rules in the workplace. In other words, we begin to think and behave like our parents.

An example of a positive parent state of mind is when they take the time to teach someone about a specific process that is commonly used. On the other hand, a critical parent would yell or angrily tell people what to do. Statements like, "Because I said so," "I always have to babysit my team," or speaking in a condescending manner are all examples of what we might hear from a critical parent.

THE ADULT

The healthiest state of mind is the *adult.* The adult is always rational and logical. Adults express themselves objectively and inquisitively while still factoring in their social-emotional intelligence. The thought process of the adult includes statements such as "What do you think?" "How can we do this better?" or "What are the alternatives?"

Three States of Mind

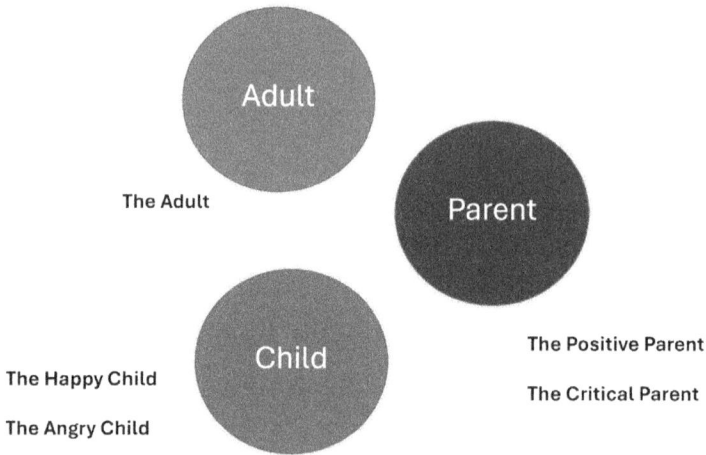

Adult

The Adult

Parent

Child

The Positive Parent

The Happy Child

The Critical Parent

The Angry Child

Avoid the Hook!

Take a moment and consider how many times your Parent, Adult, and Child states of mind emerge each day. We can quickly fluctuate between the three states depending on the situation. Take, for example, the following common problem. You decide to meet with Bob, one of your direct reports who uncharacteristically has come to work late several times in the past three weeks. Since this behavior is not typical of Bob, you want to explore to better understand the change in his behavior.

Within minutes of sharing your concern about his late attendance, Bob folds his arms, slumps in the chair, and says, "What's the big deal? The place isn't going to shut down because I came in a few minutes late!" The more you try to explore, the more defensive he becomes, as seen by his lack of eye contact, folding his arms, and talking over you. "You know, as soon as you became a manager, you started walking around here with your nose in the air and always talking on the phone. Maybe things would be better around here if you started doing your job!"

At that moment, his Angry Child is trying to *hook* you. Metaphorically speaking, they cast a fishing line trying to hook you in their manipulative rant. What happens to the relationship if you get hooked? Typically, you become the Critical Parent, or you jump in the sandbox with them. Your response may sound something like, "As long as you work for me, you better start showing up on time." Or, "No one talks to me like that, so you better be quiet!" With the hook soundly in place, the relationship has now become adversarial.

When speaking to Bob, it is important to use effective communication skills and approach him as an Adult to establish Adult–Adult interaction. However, it is crucial to remember that you cannot control Bob's thoughts, feelings, or behavior, only your own. Even if Bob reacts as an Angry Child, it is important to remain a Calm Adult. Staying in control of your own emotions will help you maintain a professional relationship with Bob.

Laser-Focused Listening

Our survey and other research show that one major complaint individual contributors have with their bosses is that they do not listen to them.[5] This is not surprising since we teach people how to speak more often than we teach people how to listen. This leaves many direct reports feeling unheard, which leads to frustration and disengagement from their boss. Highly effective leaders recognize the difference between hearing words and listening with their ears, eyes, and heart.

What other reasons exist besides being trained not to listen? When we ask this question in our workshops, the responses can fill a large flip chart. Leaders' intentions are good, but like all people, respectful listening remains a behavioral blind spot for many.

Additionally, leaders today typically wear multiple hats. From problem-solving to developing direct reports to managing budgets, they quickly learn *task-switching* (the old term for multitasking), and herein lies a problem. The brain finds it difficult to do more than one cognitive task at a time, even though you think it can.[6] Furthermore, when consistently switching tasks throughout the day, you lose up to 40 percent of productivity. When it is time to listen, stop switching tasks physically and mentally.

We also suggest that leaders inquire and listen with curiosity. Far too often, a leader meets with a direct report to discuss a project, and immediately, the leader begins the conversation by sharing their ideas, perspective, and how they believe things should proceed. The leader has just predisposed the message. Put yourself in the shoes of the direct report. Their subconscious thoughts might be, "Sounds like my boss's mind is made up," or "Who am I to argue with my boss." The creative and collaborative dialogue is diminished. Instead, try to speak last.

When you find yourself struggling with distraction, and you want to build your listening muscle, there is a simple LASER acronym you can follow: Listen, Ask, Summarize, Empathically Respond.

Listen respectfully, which requires additional elements to the skill of active listening. This is when you and the other individual come to a clear understanding of what is being said. You want to recognize the communicator's thoughts (the actual words being said), emotions, meanings, and nonverbal messages. Once identified, paraphrase what you think the communicator is saying to confirm that you understand correctly. *"If I hear you correctly, you agree to make the changes to the document?"*

Listen Respectfully

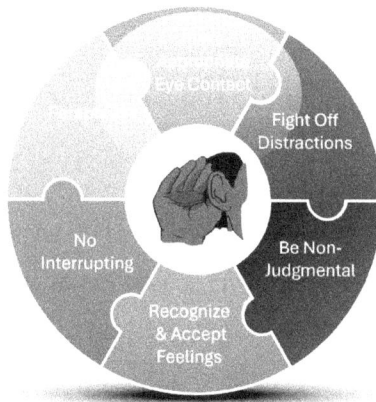

Ask exploratory questions about the communicator's thoughts, feelings, ideas, etc. This is when you gather as much information as possible to understand the person best. View exploratory questions like a picture puzzle developing in front of you. Each question you ask is another piece of the puzzle forming. Asking exploratory questions engages the person in a collaborative dialogue instead of the tell-and-sell approach. *"That is an interesting idea; tell me more about it."*

Summarize for clarity after your question. Once you identify the speaker's thoughts, emotions, meaning, and nonverbal messages, it is time to summarize to confirm that you understand correctly. A couple of phrases you might use include, "So let me see if I understand you," "It appears that what you are looking for is X," and "In the end, the most important things to you are Y and Z."

Empathically **R**esponding is the final step in the LASER acronym, and it is often the most challenging for leaders. Remember that empathy is not turned on and off like a light switch. It must come from the heart and be genuine. Also, direct reports do not want your sympathy (to feel *for* them); they want your empathy (to feel *with* them). "It sounds like you had a rough time last night."

A Final Word About Empathy . . .

Jamil Zaki's book, *The War for Kindness: Building Empathy in a Fractured World*, presents a deeper understanding of empathy and the need for more of it in these chaotic and tumultuous times.[7] In our workshops, we often ask about the definition of empathy. It is interesting to hear the numerous ways people define such a significant skill of humankind. Regardless of your definition, human beings are hardwired with the capacity to be empathetic. We learn, through our experiences, to build our level of empathy. Some people have a high degree of empathy, whereas others have very little.

Empathy has been studied for decades. Recently, empathy has been broken down into three categories:

Cognitive empathy: Relates to thinking about and imagining how a person feels. It helps keep the communication door open to facilitate a genuine connection with the person.

Emotional empathy: Relates to your ability to feel what the other person is feeling. Putting yourself in their shoes helps build an emotional bond with the other person.

Compassionate empathy: Relates to the combination of cognitive and emotional empathy that drives you to take some type of supportive and helpful action.

Regardless of the type of empathy you demonstrate, it will help to build a positive relationship with your direct reports. We believe Oprah Winfrey had her thumb on the pulse of leadership when she said, "Leadership is about empathy. It is about having the ability to relate to and connect with people for the purpose of inspiring and empowering their lives."[8]

Every reader recognizes the importance communication plays in our personal and professional lives. Empathetic communication is the vehicle that connects us. What was once considered a soft skill is now considered a hard science. Your basic communication skills are insufficient in today's workplace. With new communication technology and more sophisticated workers, leaders need to advance their communication skills. If leaders continue to use antiquated vehicles, they will have difficulty making genuine connections.

Insights

Your direct reports want you to . . .

- treat them as Adults.
- take the time to listen to them with LASER accuracy.
- constantly demonstrate empathy.

CHAPTER 7

Manage the Tension of Conflict

It's obvious you don't like conflict, but please address the employees' poor performance.

When Keith was in his twenties, he had a roommate named Ron, and even though their careers took them down different paths, they remained close friends. Since they both came from Jewish backgrounds, and since Ron had two children around the same age as Keith's children, each one invited the other's family to their children's Bar (for males) and Bat (for females) Mitzvahs. As is the custom in Judaism, when a Jewish boy or girl reaches the age of thirteen, they celebrate becoming a man or woman by participating in a Shabbat service at their local synagogue. This involves reading from the Torah and is traditionally followed up with a celebratory party for friends and family members.

A couple of years later, however, it dawned on Keith that his family had not received an invitation to Ron's second son's Bar Mitzvah. The more he thought about this, the more upset he felt at being shunned for no apparent reason. For those not raised in a Jewish culture, it's hard to explain why these events are so meaningful; they are far more than a mere birthday celebration.

For several days Keith wracked his brain for why he hadn't been invited. To his knowledge, he didn't recall having a quarrel or misunderstanding with Ron. Maybe the invitation got lost in the mail? Or perhaps the two men were not as close as Keith thought? Keith's mind gravitated toward the latter option.

We'll let Keith tell the story from here.

> In the months that followed, I found myself pulling away from Ron. I did not return his calls or invitations to exercise together as I licked my wounds from being left out of this important event. After all, I included him and his family in both my children's celebrations. Any rationalization I tried did little to subside the anger I felt.
>
> Finally, after almost a year of giving Ron the cold shoulder, I decided to practice what I preach and discuss the situation with him. We agreed to meet at the gym. As the treadmill increased to a slow jog, I turned to Ron and told him how hurt I had been and lamented about feeling rejected. As the story unfolded and I vented my pent-up anger, a large smile spread across Ron's face, and he started to laugh. This only irritated me more, and my agitation led me to become emotionally hijacked.

Sensing I was close to my breaking point, Ron calmly looked at me and said, "Keith, I didn't invite you to my son's Bar Mitzvah because he didn't have one!" From there, he explained the personal reasons that had led his family to make this decision.

As my pace on the treadmill continued to climb, my heart sank. I was stunned, and an immediate wave of guilt washed over me. I thought of all the times I had avoided my friend over the past year—all because of a misunderstanding and my unwillingness to communicate.

I had avoided my friend for months and created an entire story in my head that was not true. By doing so, the anger and hurt feelings played like an endless symphony in my mind. Why? Because I did the very thing I advise the leaders I coach not to do! I avoided conflict and having a difficult conversation.

Why Is There So Much Conflict?

Historically, humankind has been in wars and conflicts for centuries. Other primates behave similarly to humans regarding conflict: battles between species, killing one another, and other forms of conflict. This begs the question: Are we hardwired to be in conflict? The answer to the question is yes. When the brain interprets a situation as a threat, the central nervous system releases hormones to prepare the body to defend itself, the fight-or-flight response.[1]

As long as people are trying to coexist, conflict is inevitable. Our differing values, beliefs, and opinions are a constant breeding ground for misunderstandings. Conflict can take on many forms, some leading to positive outcomes while others are devastating. Regardless, our professional belief is that the basis of all conflicts and disagreements is rooted in differences of opinion. We all have opinions about something. When one's opinions are different from another's opinions, conflict may well result.

Unfortunately, when most people think of conflict, they conjure up thoughts of fights, battles, and other uncomfortable images. Rarely considered is how conflict can lead to cohesiveness, improve group effectiveness, and bring about positive change. However, it can be easier to embrace when conflict is seen as a simple difference of opinion.

To simplify the concept of conflict, it is helpful to metaphorically see yourself as a tree. In the rooted underground lies your deep core beliefs. From your core beliefs, sprout your values (integrity, principles, and ethics) that develop in the trunk section of your tree. And from there lies everyday opinions that exist in the branched portion of the tree.

The key to managing or resolving conflicts is to understand each conflicting party's core beliefs. However, since conflict begins in the branches' location of the metaphoric tree, many people remain stuck in that area. Often, this is because of the emotional state associated with our opinions. In fact, it's these negative emotions that hinder people from resolving or managing their conflict successfully.

Conflict can happen with simple differences. For example, if I asked you to name the greatest basketball player to play the game and you replied LeBron James while I responded with Michael Jordan, we are in conflict. Is there any problem at this point? No.

We are unlikely to be in danger of coming to blows, but we are still in a conflict. The real challenge arises when our frustration levels increase. As this happens, we ante up our attempts to influence one another. With high emotions, we may even find ourselves resorting to personal attacks. "You don't think LeBron is better than Michael because you are old and stuck in your ways!" Suddenly, the conflict has become ugly and personal.

This simple example is what typically happens when people are in conflict. A benign difference of opinion can turn into an emotional tirade that leads to hurt and frustration. Essentially, conflicts come and go. It is the negative emotions that people try to avoid. For leaders, this avoidance at the workplace (and home) can have many unintended consequences.

The Financial Cost of Conflict

One consequence of not managing or resolving conflict is the cost to an organization. Picture a company with 360 direct reports. Let's say ten minutes per day per person is lost due to some conflict. This would come out to be 3,600 minutes per day, 300 hours a week, and 15,600 hours lost yearly to conflict. Assuming the average wage and benefit rate was $30 per hour, this organization's total cost of conflict would be around $468,000! Think about that: only ten minutes of conflict per day with a cost of close to a half million dollars to the organization.

Although one can manipulate the numbers to make a case, the point should be clear. There are tremendous costs associated with unresolved conflicts. Workers, teams, customers, and the entire organization are all affected. Once identified, it is incumbent upon leaders to deal with an ongoing conflict in the team. If not, the effects of conflict will spread throughout the team like a contagious virus.

Given how people perceive conflict so differently, it is understandable why so many leaders avoid it. They pretend it does not exist as the proverbial elephant sits in the corner of the room. In fact, one of the survey questions asked, "If you were asked to complete an honest, anonymous assessment of your supervisor/ manager, what would be the main opportunity for improvement you would recommend?" The number one response was to help managers embrace conflict, followed by encouraging them to have difficult conversations.

Every leader wants a high-performing department or team. But as workers and teams interact, conflicts will inevitably emerge. That said, ineffective and harmful responses to conflict can be avoided, and effective and beneficial responses can be learned. President Ronald Reagan said it right, "Peace is not the absence of conflict; it is the ability to handle conflict by peaceful means."[2] Since conflict is inevitable, handling conflict peacefully begins by recognizing that how a person responds to conflict is essential.

Simply put, there are destructive and constructive ways to deal with conflict. In the works of Sal Capobianco, PhD; Mark Davis, PhD; Linda Kraus, PhD; and in their development of the Conflict Dynamics Profile (CDP), they identified people's constructive responses, destructive responses, and hot buttons. The CDP is an excellent tool to help leaders identify the behaviors associated with conflict and their hot buttons.[3]

CONSTRUCTIVE RESPONSES	DESTRUCTIVE RESPONSES
Perspective Taking	Winning at All Costs
Creating Solutions	Displaying Anger
Expressing Emotions	Demeaning Others
Reaching Out	Retaliating
Reflective Thinking	Avoiding
Delay Responding	Yielding
Adapting	Hiding Emotions
	Self-Criticizing

If you have not taken the assessment, review the list of both responses and identify the ones you gravitate to. Pay close attention to your destructive responses. Now, think about how your direct reports might perceive you when you respond in the manner you selected.

Mistrust, Competition, and Personalities

One of our favorite activities in the leadership workshops we conduct is based on a game theory called "Win as Many Points as You Can." Once divided into partners and groups, the objective is to win as many points as possible by laying down either an X or O chip. Points are scored according to a matrix with all possible combinations and played for ten rounds. If, for example, everyone in the group chooses X, then everyone loses one point. If all choose O, everyone wins one point. If a mixture of Xs and Os is on the table, those who played X win more points than those who chose the O chip. Table discussion is not allowed except during three bonus rounds where points are multiplied three, five, and ten times.

Watching this play is fascinating. It is not unusual for participants to recognize that everyone wins points by choosing the O chip. However, to increase their **individual** chance of winning points, they choose the X chip, often at the expense of others. During the bonus rounds, when table talk is allowed, it is not unusual that participants promise one another to lay down the O chip when, in fact, they lay down the X chip. You can only imagine what transpires. The mistrust among the group immediately emerges. The activity is lively as participants experience significant learning points.

Besides the mistrust among the players, the innate need to win at all costs even if it means lying to others, quickly surfaces through this activity. What follows in the debrief of the activity is how competitive Americans have learned to become and the impact it has on the workplace. America has become a hypercompetitive society, and it plays out in all areas of life.

There is a powerful need to *be the best*. Silver medals are a mark of falling short and a constant reminder that we could have done more. For many, there is a genuine belief that competition is one of the most effective ways to foster growth and maturity. Competition is woven into the fabric of our society. From Little League Baseball to high school and collegiate sports to playing golf with friends on Sunday mornings, we enjoy competing, and winning is the ultimate goal.

In his book *No Contest: The Case Against Competition*, Alfie Kohn notes, "The case for competition is based on four central myths. The first is that competition is an unavoidable fact. The second is that competition motivates us to do our best. Third is the assertion that contests are the best way to have a good time. And the fourth myth is that competition builds character."[4] In Kohn's opinion, all these assertions are false. Contrary to popular belief, it is *not* human nature to be competitive. In many cultures, competition as we know it does not exist: Zuni Indians; Iroquois Indians; the BaThonga in South Africa, Kenya; Aborigines; the Kibbutz; and many Asian countries.

Since competition is a learned behavior, the need to win develops through conditioning and influence. The type of competition found in our country is what Alfie Kohn calls *structural competition*. As Kohn would suggest, structural competition involves a win-lose framework (like the "Win as Many Points as You Can" activity). My success depends on your failure. Basically, there is a fifty-fifty chance of being a winner or a loser. Thus, we have been conditioned to intentionally compete as a survivable mechanism. And when we compete, we do so out of a primary concern for our own welfare. If the group's welfare is more important, then cooperation naturally follows. In doing so, we lose our ability to empathize, feel less inclined to help, and are more mistrustful and aggressive.

We know that we are challenging conventional wisdom. This conversation drives a good deal of pushback in our workshops. One of our goals in using this activity is to bring awareness of the importance of cooperation. In other words, cooperate within your teams and organization and compete against your external competitors. "How do we win?" is a question many ask. By being the best you can be, provide the highest quality of products (services, etc.) and customer experience in the most ethical manner. We need to move from *structural competition* to *cooperative competition,* also known as *coopetition.*[5]

When Personalities Collide

Perhaps you have taken a personality or behavioral assessment such as Myers-Briggs or DiSC. No doubt you experienced some personal surprises along the way. "So that's why I respond the way I do!" you might have said to yourself. With this new understanding, you recognize why a conflict exists between you and a direct report on your team. It is not that they are a negative contrarian, but because they process information differently from you.

Take the difference between extroverts and introverts. Extroverts who monopolize team meetings may assume that the quiet (introverted) people in the meeting do not have anything meaningful to contribute. Meanwhile, the introverts feel like extroverts dominate the conversation without giving time for others to process the information.

Consider, for example, someone extremely time-bound will always arrive ten minutes early for the start of a meeting. If it starts at 8:30, they will be there at 8:20. By 8:25, they might notice the room is half full and have already written off the rest of the attendees as *late*. But those who arrive at 8:35 run on their own internal clock and get to the meeting close to the start time. These opposing preferred behaviors can easily lead to conflicts.

The first time we attempted to design and develop a new training course, Matt and I experienced a severe conflict. Being a linear and sequential thinker, my approach is a step-by-step method that begins with an outline. From there, I would create the Participant Guide; the last piece is the development of the supporting PowerPoints. On the other hand, Matt is a creative and big-picture thinker who is less constrictive in his approach.

Picture us sitting at a table, ready to delve into our first creation. Matt started with, "OK, let's get started. Now, the first PowerPoint should—" I abruptly interrupted and said, "The first PowerPoint?! What do you mean by the first PowerPoint? We need to start at the beginning with the first page of the Participant Guide." The argument lasted about fifteen minutes before we realized we had opposing personality styles. Once recognized, our emotions subsided, and we gained a new understanding of one another. From that time forward, when we develop new materials, we start by declaring which *style* we will utilize.

To be human is to be in conflict. There are multiple reasons for conflicts, as there are multiple approaches to resolving or managing conflicts effectively. High-performing leaders recognize this, can adopt constructive responses to conflict, and utilize the appropriate method to mitigate conflicts.

Insights

Your direct reports want you to . . .

- deal with and manage conflict in a timely manner.
- practice constructive responses when in conflict.
- recognize and accept personality differences when in conflict.

CARE front Instead of *CON* front

*Be more sensitive to people's needs
when communicating.*

Managing conflict effectively requires a blend of cognitive and behavioral changes. It may come in recognizing the positive benefits of conflict or simply identifying one's hot buttons. It requires an understanding that some conflicts cannot be resolved and must be managed. Take, for example, the topic of politics. If you are a diehard Democrat, it is going to be tough to have a substantive conversation with someone who is a strong Republican. The differences are just too significant. You probably learned it is best to agree to disagree to preserve the relationship.

Chapter 6 emphasized the analogy of *keeping the communication door open*. When you confront someone about their behavior, some see it as a threat or opposition, and the communication door closes. Instead of *CON*fronting the person, *CARE*front them. *CARE*front is an acronym:

Control your emotions

Assess your beliefs

Rediscover common ground/goals

Explore for solutions and agreement

When you *CARE*front a person, the approach is less antagonistic, which leads to less defensiveness, allowing for a collaborative conversation between adults.

The CAREfront Model

4 **E**xplore for Possible Solutions/Agreement

3 **R**ediscover Common Ground/Goals

2 **A**ssess Beliefs

1 **C**ontrol Your Emotions

Control Your Emotions

The driving energy behind conflict is the emotions and feelings associated with it. Typically, a conflict begins with a feeling of frustration, which, left unchecked, can soon result in anger. The problem arises from how a person deals with their anger. In Chapter

7, we identified constructive and destructive responses to conflict. Some people yell, some become violent, and others can *talk it out*. Expressing emotions in a constructive manner is an effective way to manage conflict. Specifically, regulate your emotional state by controlling what we call your *stinking thinking*.

It is helpful to recognize the thought process to understand how one's stinking thinking affects behavior. When a situation is experienced, it sets off a mental process in the brain. For example, imagine someone punches you in the nose. Your response might be to hit them back. But there is more to the process. Once receiving the punch, your brain processes a thought, feeling, and belief in milliseconds.

Thought: "Hey, this guy just punched me in the nose!"

Feeling: "That hurts."

Belief: "He can't do that to me; I'm going to punch him back!"

Now, imagine your response if you received a punch from the world's heavyweight champion. After you wake up and hold an icepack to your head for several hours, your likely response might be to call your lawyer. But let's use a final illustration. Imagine you receive a punch to the nose, but this time, it's from a four-year-old boy. You are probably not reaching for your phone to call your lawyer.

Notice your different responses with each scenario. You have been punched in the nose three different times, and yet your response changed with each instance. How you thought and felt about the situation radically changed with each example. In life, we encounter numerous situations that are out of our control. However, what we can control is how we think about the situations.

Imagine, for example, that we tell you a joke. Hopefully, you *think* it's funny and *feel* happy, and your *response* is to laugh. Imagine someone offered you $5,000 *not* to laugh at our joke. At that point, unless we are hilarious, we guess that you will win the bet. Upon analysis, you continued to *think* in ways that prevented you from laughing, allowing you to win the bet; you controlled your emotional state.

Therefore, if you want to change a negative feeling or behavior, it is vital to zero in on the thoughts associated with your feelings and behavior. At that point, you can challenge the thought. Doing so requires you to determine if the thought is rational or irrational. Typically, stinking thinking results from irrational thinking and is not based on facts.

Some common examples might include:

- Labeling: "All politicians are X."
- Mind reading: "I know why they did that."
- Magnification: "I waited all day for your call."
- Catastrophizing: "I'm going to get fired."
- Should/Shouldn't: "I shouldn't have made so many mistakes."

What is helpful is to learn a psychological technique called cognitive restructuring. One such restructuring approach is called *reframing*. Reframing is a technique that allows you to look at a negative situation differently. It is not a lesson in positive thinking but a technique to rethink the event or situation you face neutrally or benignly. By doing so, you can move the information to the logical part of the brain, allowing a more rational perspective to emerge.

Reframing

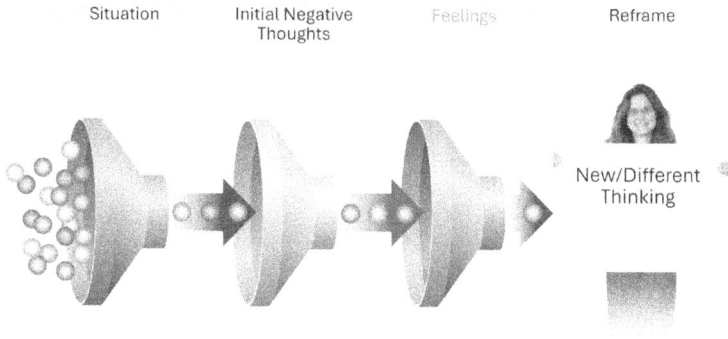

Situation — Initial Negative Thoughts — Feelings — Reframe — New/Different Thinking

Reframing is one of the most effective techniques in dealing with adversity, stressors, and conflicts. In fact, most people use some form of reframing daily. Let's say a loved one passes away after a long battle with a debilitating illness.

People will say things like:

- "They are no longer suffering."
- "They are in a better place."
- "They lived a long life."

Keep in mind, there are no right or wrong reframes. Whatever works for you is best. Your ability to reframe your stinking thinking—in this case, by maintaining a rational and logical perspective—is critical to managing emotions.

Several years ago, a hardware store owner shared with us some of the feelings he experienced when he found out two of his cashiers had stolen and embezzled his store out of $300,000 dollars over a ten-year period. He had every right to be angry and hurt by the circumstances he faced. But as he continued with the story, he looked at us and off-handedly remarked, "Well, that's the bad news." We looked at him and said, "You mean there is good news to this story?" He smiled and said, "Well, at least I got rid of two partners I didn't know I had!" This is a perfect example of reframing at its best.

The more you practice the reframing technique, the easier it becomes to manage your emotional state. When should you apply reframing? Anytime you begin to feel negative. For example, say to yourself, "I'm feeling angry. I must be having angry thoughts." At that point, identify the stinking thinking thought, challenge the rationality of it, and then reframe it.

Reframe Others

At times, your direct reports have come to you with misfortunes that interfere with their performance at work. Since the direct report's performance is affected, it is essential for you to address the issue. In doing so, it may be helpful to use the reframing technique. Reframing others is a more advanced technique that, when used effectively, provides leaders with a tool to connect with their direct reports empathically.

Begin by asking them to describe the conflicting issue. Be sure to listen respectfully as you recognize and validate their feelings. Explore and link any past problems triggering the current situation (for example, a past conflict with the person). Remember, people tend to *magnify* or *catastrophize* the story they tell you. If this happens, help them identify their distorted thoughts and beliefs. Their thinking could be dichotomous: "I lost everything when my computer crashed." Or "Nothing ever goes smoothly." To refocus the person, restate their thought and place emphasis on the dichotomous word. For example: "You lost *everything*." Or "*Nothing* ever goes smoothly." Last, use metaphors, allegories, and analogies in the discussion to convey understanding. "When confronted by Pam, you felt ambushed." Or "When you heard what happened, it was like being punched in the gut."

The following story from Keith will help you better understand the application of helping someone else reframe a situation.

> One morning, as I preboarded a plane to Chicago, I took my aisle seat, one seat in front of a lady who had a window seat behind me. Seconds later, I heard her phone ring, and upon her answering it, she began to cry. Not for seconds but a resounding cry that lasted for several minutes.
>
> Finally, after hearing her despair, I got up and took the middle seat next to her. I put my hand on her shoulder, and she collapsed into my chest, weeping. I asked her what had happened, and she told me she'd just learned that her thirty-eight-year-old brother had died suddenly from a massive heart attack.
>
> As she vented, I listened reflectively and with empathy. Since she was in an immediate and unfortunate crisis, I searched my brain for a suitable reframe. Waiting for the right moment to interject, I presented the following. "Your brother's unexpected death is clearly a shock and causing you tremendous pain. You

mentioned that you have been the apple of his eye for many years and had a remarkably close relationship. You were his confidant and mentor."

Once she agreed, I then asked, "What do you suppose would have happened to your brother if you had died unexpectedly?"

"Oh my gosh!" She exclaimed. "He would have freaked out. There is no way he could have handled it. He would have been devastated without me around."

I looked at her and said, "He will never experience that pain."

And with a deep sigh, she slowly regained her composure.

I did not do anything remarkable. I listened reflectively with my ears, eyes, and heart. Without discounting or dismissing the tragic loss of her brother, I did, however, empathically provide a reframe that gave her brother's death new meaning.

After we landed, I waited for my ride at the same place this lady was standing. She hugged me and said, "Thank you, you are definitely going to heaven."

I replied, "It all depends on who you ask!" We laughed.

Assess Beliefs

One of the keys to managing conflict effectively is understanding your and the other person's core beliefs. This information is used to discover the actual differences between you and them and help you negotiate a solution. Once you are clear about what is important to you and what you need and want, ask the other person the same question. This is best accomplished by using some of the communication skills discussed earlier and by taking their perspective.

Perspective-taking is an excellent technique for helping people better understand each other's beliefs, wants, and needs. Simply put, perspective-taking refers to your ability to see a situation from a different point of view. It's putting yourself in another person's shoes. This understanding allows you to find common ground that leads to resolution or better conflict management.

Let's use the illustration of parenting a four-year-old child. Every parent has their personal beliefs that dictate how they discipline their children. Let's say you believe that spanking children is the best form of discipline. Now, think of how difficult it might be to influence someone who opts for nonphysical methods of discipline, such as time-outs. What would you say to persuade them that your viewpoint was correct? Now, reverse roles. Place yourself in the position of someone who believes time-out is the most effective form of discipline. Now, think what it would be like to convince someone who believes that spanking is the best method of disciplining children that time-out is more effective.

This is an activity we use in our workshops when teaching perspective-taking. When debriefing the participants, it is not uncommon that some people refuse to take the perspective of the spanking method due to their abusive histories. This is a significant point. Due to people's beliefs and convictions, seeing the other person's point of view often becomes challenging. However, successfully placing yourself in the other person's shoes and assessing their beliefs does *not* mean you agree with them. It simply means you better understand their thoughts and feelings. You might take issue with the conclusions they have drawn, but you can understand their point of view, allowing you to be open to finding an agreeable solution to the conflict.

Rediscover Common Ground/Goals

Conflict exists because of the differences between people. Therefore, finding common ground with others and reducing the existing differences is essential. Besides the ability to take the person's perspective, another helpful technique is *blending*. Blending involves communicating signals to one another that convey similarities, openness, and connection. We can blend visually, verbally, with tone of voice, and even with the words we use. Finding ways to blend with the person reduces defensiveness and allows people to see the similarities that drive a genuine connection.

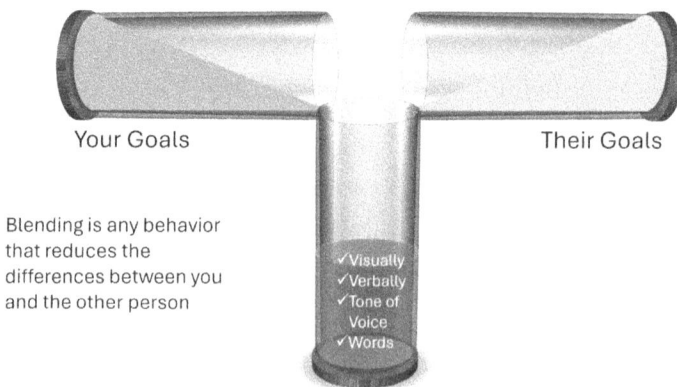

Blending
When in Conflict Find Common Ground by "Blending"

Your Goals

Their Goals

Blending is any behavior that reduces the differences between you and the other person

✓ Visually
✓ Verbally
✓ Tone of Voice
✓ Words

A couple of years ago, Matt and I were checking into a Dallas hotel to provide training and coaching to a client. I inquired at the front desk about being transported to the meeting place in the morning. They directed me to Dave, the head concierge, at the end of the counter. As I moved down the counter, Dave said, "I hear you guys are from the Detroit area!" I nodded, and he continued saying he went to college near Detroit. "Whereabouts?" I asked. "Bowling Green in Ohio." I perked up and told him I had as well. Although a few years older than me, he explained he played football there. I laughed and said, "So did I!" For the next twenty minutes, much to Matt's annoyance, we shared football stories, discussed coaches, and even sang the first verse of the school song!

As we were chatting away, a gentleman waiting in line to check in leaned over and asked, "Hey! You guys from Detroit?" As I turned to say yes, in unison, he said, "Keith!" and I said, "Jeff!" Once again, I had made an unexpected connection, this time with an old basketball teammate from my neighborhood. Finding common ground unexpectedly can be fun.

When people get along, they naturally blend by mirroring each other via body posture, facial expressions, and tone of voice. Think about your body posture and how you would respond to one of your peers at work who just won a great deal of money in Las Vegas, as opposed to another person who told you about the unexpected death of a close relative. No doubt your eye contact, voice animation, and approach would change based on these two very different interactions.

As natural as it is to do this kind of emotional mirroring, you must use caution in the workplace. Be careful *not* to blend when one of your direct reports is emotionally upset. When a conflict becomes heated, you will likely talk faster and louder to influence one another. This is the time for you to speak a bit slower and dial down your volume compared to the other person. Remember, your goal is to find commonalities and similarities, eventually making resolving or managing the conflict more manageable.

Explore for Possible Solutions and Agreement

*CARE*fronting people can be tricky, and the solutions may not always be apparent. You may need to brainstorm ways to link the possible solutions to the identified common interests and goals. When doing so, follow these three recommendations.

1. First, collaborate when creating a list of possible solutions. Follow the brainstorming rules, and do not evaluate the ideas until you have completed the list.

2. Next, combine your ideas to find a workable solution. If the other person is highly resistant, allow them to voice their ideas first. The focus should be on the solutions, not what happened in the past.

3. Then, collaboratively decide on how to execute the solutions, and be sure to assess the progress of your solutions by scheduling follow-up meetings.

Challenging Conversation

During times of conflict, we become brilliant storytellers. Typically, an entire story is concocted that consists of characters, a plot, a villain and victim, and an ending. The characters are well-defined in roles and personalities, and the outcome always fits your desires and motivation. Unfortunately, the story is based on distortions and other irrational thoughts.

The victim's story has the same basic theme: "I'm good, and the other person is bad and evil!" The victims view themselves as helpless and innocent. They often say, "Hey, it's not my fault." Or "This always happens to me."

On the other hand, the villain's story is to cast blame, find fault, and prove the other person's unequivocal wrong. When you eventually perfect this story, the other characters pale in comparison to Attila the Hun. Typical statements of a villain are: "If he had half a brain, he wouldn't have done that." "My manager is a cold-hearted jerk who never understands me." "I can't believe he did that to me!"

This last statement perfectly describes Keith's challenge with his friend Ron when he thought Ron had excluded him from his son's Bar Mitzvah. By making Ron the villain, Keith created a story that was not true. He took a series of fake-fact tidbits and interpreted them as factual information. When you abandon the traditional *victim and villain* storytelling, you can open up to creating a new and realistic story based on accurate information.

There was a popular detective TV show in the 1970s called *Columbo*. Peter Falk, the actor playing the detective, was a master at minimizing defensive behavior that eventually led to solving the crime.

His approach to people was disarming as he communicated tentatively in what we call *Columbo language.*

- "Perhaps you were unaware . . ."

- "In my opinion . . ."
- "My perception is . . . and it doesn't mean I'm right . . ."

Approaching conversations in a way such as the preceding examples reduces defensiveness and portrays your uncertain view and doubt, which allows the other person to feel safe.

Another technique is to use language with your team that demonstrates your flexibility: Focus on the person's behavior, not the person. It's saying things like, "When I see you arrive late to a meeting, I get a little upset," versus "You obviously have a problem with the start time of the meeting, which really bugs me!"

One of the challenges when one person is sharing a story with another is that the other person may become defensive. As discussed earlier, when that happens, the logical brain shuts down. Becoming a detached listener will help you remain focused and objective in conflict. Detached listening requires you to disengage from the emotional part of the message. This is not easy to accomplish due to the feelings related to the conflict. When achieved, however, it helps you stay focused on the issues.

A simple and sincere apology works wonders. The last thing frustrating people expect is for you to agree with them. Therefore, your best response is to agree with their feelings and let go of whether their facts are right or wrong.

Last, accept the person's criticism to diffuse the conversation. When you try to explain why something happened or did not happen, the other person will continue to press on until they feel understood.

As we have repeatedly mentioned, conflict can be productive, healthy, and positive when establishing and maintaining a *CARE*fronting approach with your direct reports and teams.

Insights

Your direct reports want you to . . .

- CAREfront instead of CONfront them.

- manage your emotions by using the reframing technique.

- use the Colombo approach.

CHAPTER 9

Provide Appropriate Feedback

It would be nice to receive more appreciation
when I do well and focus less on my mistakes.

For ninety-nine correct things and one mistake, think of what goes through your mind when your leader comes up to you and says, "Hey, I need to see you in my office this afternoon. I have some constructive criticism I would like to give you." Unless you are the rare exception, you immediately begin thinking about what you did or didn't do. You mentally brace yourself for the difficult or harsh feedback you will receive. Even when a person hears constructive criticism, it tends to conjure up various negative emotions and feelings. The brain reacts and moves into protective mode.

Specifically, if you are about to deliver feedback that requires a shift in your direct report's behavior, you must communicate it in a way that keeps both you and your direct report open and receptive. The term *feedback* serves multiple purposes, whether it is positive or negative. Classifying terms like *supportive* and *corrective* for feedback has a more positive tone. One is more receptive, and the communication door remains open. Supportive feedback reinforces the behavior you want to see continued. Corrective feedback refers to behavior that needs to change. Regardless of the type of feedback, it should be given with compassion and empathy.

One way to look at feedback, specifically the feedback you would give your direct report, is to view it as a gift. Consider the *gift of feedback* as a general analogy. We have been taught that when receiving a gift, it is polite to acknowledge it and thank the person. Even if the gift is something you do not like, such as the unsightly sweater your grandmother bought for you, you don't say, "This is the ugliest sweater I have ever seen!" Instead, you smile and appropriately respond with a thank you. What would happen if you responded negatively whenever you received a gift? As the soup Nazi from a *Seinfeld* episode exclaimed, "No soup [gift] for you!"[1]

A client called us to give negative feedback about one of our facilitators who provided a workshop. They liked her, but she told too many stories about herself that were irrelevant to the course topic or the class. We proceeded to have a meeting with Sue, the facilitator. We explained what the client expressed, and she was mildly defensive but took the feedback in stride. About a month later, we received similar feedback from another client about Sue's ongoing personal storytelling. Again, we had a follow-up meeting with Sue. This time, however, she immediately blamed the participants in the class for a lack of understanding and aggressively attacked us. By the end of the tirade, we calmly responded, "No need to shoot the messenger." Because Sue was so defensive and nonreceptive to feedback, we eventually felt there was no value in providing it for her. Needless to say, Sue no longer works for us.

The preceding story exemplifies what can happen when giving feedback. When feedback is interpreted as criticism, people can become defensive. Knowing that you cannot control how others decipher a message, it becomes critically important for leaders to deliver feedback that intentionally minimizes defensive reactions. It is helpful to provide feedback in an exploratory and engaging manner. If you can provide feedback in such a supportive and corrective way, it can feel like a gift—and who doesn't like getting gifts? Even if it's an "ugly Christmas sweater" that can only be worn once a year at your company's holiday party.

Many Ways Leaders Give Feedback

There are four common ways leaders give feedback. These include:

- Enthusiastic Feedback

- Critical Feedback

- Passive Feedback

- Supportive/Corrective Feedback

In our years of professional training and coaching, we have found a simple feedback exercise that has proved effective and enlightening. We begin by using a cardboard box with four tennis balls and then suggest that participants sit around a U-shaped table. From there, they are divided into four teams. Each team is asked to provide a volunteer for the exercise. The four volunteers are taken to a location that is out of sight and hearing of the other participants. The remaining members of the four teams are then briefed on their roles in the exercise.

They are told the volunteers will be brought back into the room individually. The volunteers will sit in a chair facing away from the box, which will be about ten feet behind the chair. The volunteer will then be given the four tennis balls and told to throw each of them in succession backward, over their head, and try to get them to land in the box. As each team's volunteer attempts the exercise, the volunteer will ask their team members for guidance on how well they are doing and what they need to do to improve their efforts. Each team will support their volunteers to get all four balls in the box. However, they are limited to the one assigned type of feedback they can offer.

TYPE 1: CRITICAL FEEDBACK

The first volunteer will only receive critical feedback that does not encourage or direct them but attacks their behavior. Without being personal, participants hurl criticisms such as: "That stinks!" "Wow, you are way off the mark!" or "This should be easy to do; what's your problem?"

This is to model the behavior of leaders giving negative, unhelpful feedback. Whenever this happens, the reactions from the volunteers can become quite intense! We have seen volunteers take their balls and throw them at their team members in anger or give up in disgust. One of our volunteers had thrown three balls, and after continuing to hear negative feedback, he gave up. Instead of throwing it over his shoulder, he rolled it between his legs in the general direction of the box.

When we debriefed the exercise, everyone kept asking, "With only one ball left, why did you give up and not throw it? Why did you roll it between your legs behind you?" We will never forget his answer. He replied that he had felt so diminished based on the negative feedback that he began to think there wasn't even a box behind him. He had rolled the final ball between his legs just to know if he could hear it hit the box to validate there was actually something there!

In short, trust had been broken down so much that the volunteer made a possible assumption the team was never telling him the truth. This simple illustration has some obvious real-life analogies.

TYPE 2: ENCOURAGING FEEDBACK

The next group is directed to solely provide encouraging statements like "Great job," "You're doing terrific," "What a team player," or "Keep trying."

We need to pause here and point out that this type of feedback will most likely be misunderstood. We are led to believe that encouraging feedback is what we should always be doing. However, feedback without any specifics does little to empower team members.

Volunteers who receive this type of feedback are often the quickest to throw their tennis balls, with the assumption they are doing everything they are supposed to do. Because all they hear is positive feedback, they keep throwing, never asking questions, and falsely assuming they are doing a great job. We often refer to this feedback as *drive-by feedback*. It's the classic story of the leader walking by the direct report, patting them on the back, saying "Great job," and continuing to move along. While this might feel good, the one receiving this type of response lacks direct feedback on what part of that project was performed well and which areas could be improved. Encouraging feedback can be a great motivator and source of energy for people. However, it lacks the required information on how to achieve a desired goal or perform a specific task. Although encouraging feedback feels better than critical feedback, rarely does a ball find the box.

TYPE 3: PASSIVE FEEDBACK

The third example we share is those who give passive feedback. Here, we instruct groups to provide no direction on how their tennis ball–throwing teammate can improve. Our poor volunteer might throw balls dead center of the box or be off by a mile. In addition, the team with this assigned feedback cannot provide motivational comments like, "That's good!" "That ball almost went in." Even the nonverbal reactions are supplied with a little more than a shrug of indifference. The feedback is meant to be vague and ambiguous. And as you might expect, this type of feedback leaves us with many frustrated volunteers.

This illustration reminds us of disengaged leaders who are not focused on supporting their direct reports. They are constantly multitasking and never focused on the present. As a result, they fail to provide the care and support their teams so desperately need to succeed.

TYPE 4: SUPPORTIVE AND CORRECTIVE FEEDBACK

This final group of team members is the whole package. They allow themselves the ability to give corrective feedback and positive and supportive insight. As you might guess, this approach yielded the most promising results during our exercise. Statements like, "Your last ball was two feet to the left of the box" or "You overshot the box by eighteen inches" naturally provide volunteers with the necessary tools to make the required adjustments.

Supportive/corrective feedback is used to reinforce effective and desirable behavior. It lets others know when you are pleased with their behavior and helps them see specific areas where they can improve. In short, it sets them up for success. Expectations are clear, positive behaviors are cheered, and performance is met with helpful feedback.

Those Difficult Conversations

Picture the following. You reviewed the recent 360-assessment report on Zack, a leader who reports to you. To your surprise, his eight direct reports rated him low (average 2.5 out of 5 rating) throughout the entire assessment. In contrast, Zack rated himself a 4.2 in most assessment areas. Clearly, there is a disconnect between how Zack views himself and the feedback he is receiving from others. This needs to be addressed, but you are not looking forward to the conversation due to Zack's aggressive communication style.

You would not be alone in your discomfort in having a difficult discussion with a direct report with a style such as Zack's. In our survey, for example, almost 20 percent agreed that leaders avoiding difficult conversations would be one of the most significant opportunities for improvement. So why do leaders avoid difficult conversations?

A difficult conversation can be an emotional event that triggers negative feelings within yourself and the other person. As a leader, recognize that what hinders the working relationship more is what's *not* said. Having a transactional, emotional-free conversation at that moment is no longer an option. These challenging and emotionally charged conversations require good emotional management, social awareness, and fine-tuned communication skills. Without those three skills being intentionally practiced, the conversation can go south quickly.

The key to managing a difficult conversation begins with preparation and your approach to delivering the information.

The following suggestions will help you prepare for these conversations:

- Prepare yourself before having the conversation. Like a speech to be given, rehearse over and over in your head. Recognize and embrace your uncomfortable feelings as being a normal reaction. Anticipate your and the other person's hot buttons and any other issues that could close the communication door.

- How you begin the conversation is essential. You want to be a "conscious communicator" and be aware of your feelings, behaviors, and words. For example, begin an opening sentence with *I* instead of *you*. The *you* can often feel like a finger pointed at one's face. Be conscious of not using inflammatory terminology.

- Inquire and explore. This is the time to listen with the intent to understand. Remember, you both have your own stories. It is essential to remain open-minded and understand the person. Ask open-ended questions and listen reflectively.

- If the person communicates aggressively or quickly blames you, there is no need to defend yourself. In fact, the more you resist, the more they will persist. Instead, use the Five Key Questions technique we describe below.

When experiencing a strong emotional reaction, you can become emotionally hijacked. When this occurs, your emotional brain takes over the logical brain, and you no longer think rationally or logically. By asking yourself (self-talk) and answering the Five Key Questions, you help the brain regain its logical composure so that you can do what is in your best interest.

To help regain a logical perspective, ask yourself these Five Key Questions:

- What are my goals in having a conversation with this person?

- What can't I control?

- What can I control?

- What choices do I have?

- What are the possible consequences of my choice?

Let's revisit our example with Zack, the boss whose reports scored him lower than he scored himself. Knowing this could be a difficult conversation based on the difference in perceptions and his aggressive communication style, let's apply the Five Key Questions technique.

1. What are my goals in having a conversation with Zack?

    a. To help Zack recognize the perception gap in how he sees himself versus how others see him.

    b. To use this information to enhance his leadership style.

2. What can't I control?

    a. You can't control Zack's thoughts, feelings, and behaviors.

3. What can I control?

    a. You can only control your own thoughts, feelings, and behaviors.

4. What choices do I have?

    a. Referring to the PAC Model, you can approach Zack as either a Parent, Adult, or Child.

5. What are the possible consequences of my choice?

    a. If you choose to be parental, he may become angry and defensive. Is that one of your goals? If the consequences don't align with one of your goals, then most likely it's not a good choice. In contrast, if you approach Zack as an adult, you communicate calmly and help Zack identify the gap in his assessment.

Giving feedback can be challenging based on your communication style, how the person interprets your message and other variables. Recently, when presenting this material to a group of leaders at Hegira Health discussing the importance of giving feedback, a participant asked us a *why*-type question related to the issues of a negative interpretation. Our response was simple, "Because we are human." We didn't realize the CEO had entered the room quietly behind us until we heard her speak. She confirmed our response when she said, "What a perfect answer. It can keep us sane during difficult times."

Insights

Your direct reports want . . .

- ongoing supportive and corrective feedback, not constructive criticism.

- to know any concerns regarding their performance. If there are problems or challenges, share the information immediately, do not avoid or delay for months. They cannot improve what they don't know.

CHAPTER 10

Coach and Develop Direct Reports

I wish my manager took the time to understand what is important to me.

In every department and/or team, there will be *superstars* who give you 100 percent effort every day and others who provide minimal effort and are poor performers. The difference often boils down to a person's *discretionary effort.* Discretionary effort is the level of effort a direct report chooses to give at any given time. An essential job of a leader is to coach their direct reports to provide optimum performance—to inspire and enhance their discretionary effort. This is done by creating a motivating environment so the direct report feels inspired and engaged in their work.

The ability to coach direct reports is a crucial skill of high-performing leaders. They identify and capitalize on their direct reports' uniqueness and individuality to help them become more of what they are. By creating a risk-free environment that is free from retribution and by allowing mistakes to be made, leaders find ways to provide teachable moments. They consistently offer supportive and corrective feedback and offer the tools, resources, and materials for their direct reports to enhance their discretionary efforts.

Coaching is a collaborative process. Far too often, unfortunately, some leaders remain blind to this and instead convey their message through monologues that fall on deaf ears. They communicate like a parent rather than an adult (Chapter 6), telling their direct reports what they did wrong and what they need to do to remedy the situation. When we observe this behavior in our workshops, leaders believe the coaching session went well. As many studies confirm, the reality is that most managers overestimate their coaching abilities.[1]

Making the Shift from Managers to Coaches

Since coaching is an integral role of a leader, more emphasis should be on coaching and developing people. According to our survey data, approximately 25 percent of respondents said their managers don't provide ongoing coaching and development. Leaders must educate, guide, and lead people to self-discovery in our fast-paced environment instead of telling and demanding. This fundamental shift moves those who report to us from mindless obedience to approaching their leaders with their own opinions and ideas. It allows direct reports to experience more control over their work, a critical need for all workers.

For this to happen requires a significant paradigm shift in organizations and leaders. However, transitioning control to your direct reports can be challenging and risky. It becomes a balancing act for all leaders. Yet, when you are clear on your intentions and expectations and you communicate as an adult, direct reports will soon internalize this approach and come to you with their thoughts and ideas.

Effective coaching is not an event, but a part of what leaders do daily. This may come in the form of informal or formal coaching of team members. Informal coaching includes casual conversations, such as asking about a class they took or an article they read. Formal coaching may occur when meeting for a performance review or problems. While much of coaching is informal, we believe successful coaching often involves following a formal, structured, sequential process that provides a path to achieving the results you desire. The following Five Step Process will help you get there.

STEP 1: OPEN THE MEETING AND GET AN AGREEMENT

The meeting place must be determined before the coachee (the direct report) arrives for their coaching session. While a logical place might be the leader's office, you might consider having this meeting in a more neutral setting—creating a friendly and risk-free environment.

Direct reports may be nervous and anxious when they arrive at the coaching session. How you open the meeting and connect with the person can help them become more comfortable with the coaching process. Try sitting at a round table or beside one another instead of behind a desk. The desk serves as a barrier that creates an unequal playing field.

Provide a statement of comfort, such as, "Before we begin, I would like to discuss what I hope to achieve in this meeting. I intend to use this meeting as a springboard for the future . . ." Knowing the exact nature of the meeting helps reduce the team member's discomfort.

Next, set the agenda. People operate best when they clearly understand where they are going and what is expected. Say something like, "I would like us to agree on a set of objectives for this meeting. This will keep us on track during this discussion. I want to propose . . ." This statement invites them to be part of the conversation.

With a clear understanding of the meeting, you and the direct report can quickly agree by asking, "How does that sound to you? Do you have any questions or concerns about today's meeting?"

STEP 2: EXPLORE POTENTIAL CHALLENGES

Coaching sessions become the avenue to identify and uncover possible reasons for performance issues. Performance problems are typically a result of one of three areas: the direct report does not have the aptitude and skill set for the job required; they lack motivation; or there are outside factors, such as personal problems, that interfere with their jobs. It is incumbent upon the leader to uncover the reasons for the poor performance.

When faced with a technical problem, how do you approach it? Typically, you perform a fundamental root-cause analysis to understand the cause of the problem better. A similar approach is necessary to successfully understand and resolve the issues when dealing with human problems. In most cases, the leader observes symptoms of a deeper problem. Take, for example, a person who arrives at work late for several weeks. Initially, you observe their behavior, such as being late. Effective coaches need to explore and reveal the core problem. Or a metaphor we often use: It's like peeling an onion.

Peeling the Onion

Presenting Problem or Symptoms of a Deeper Problem

The Real Problem or Core Issues

If you don't have time to do it right the first time, do you have time the second, third, fourth...time?

Let Keith share a story.

> When taking a shower after playing softball, I noticed a lump in the crease of my leg and groin area. After ruling out that it was not an injury, I thought I might have had a hernia. My office was in a professional building connected to a hospital at the time. I went to see a surgeon who confirmed my self-diagnosis and said I would need surgery as soon as possible.
>
> For a second opinion, I went to see a doctor who happens to be a friend of mine. During his examination, he asked several questions, including if I was having any problems with my feet. "My feet?" I exclaimed.

> "Now that you mention it, I've been scratching quite a bit lately." Upon examining my foot, he uncovered that I had a bad case of athlete's foot that developed into an infection and traveled up my leg into a lymph node. With an antibiotic, it healed in a few days.

The story shows that the first physician did not peel the onion, whereas the second physician did. We have seen far too many leader-coaches who do not take the time to uncover the core issue. Defensively, leaders often claim "I don't have time to 'play psychologist,' I have a team to run!" Our response is always the same: If you do not take the time to do it correctly, do you have time to do it repeatedly? Performance problems, like dandelions on the lawn, will not disappear until you get to the root.

STEP 3: MANAGE DEFENSIVE BEHAVIOR

After you have *CARE*fronted (Chapter 8) someone about their performance, your direct report will respond differently. For some, what you might have pointed out may ring true, and they are quick to adjust. Others might need more time to process what you have said or internally disagree with you, so they become quiet and withdraw. Some might become aggressive and defend their performance.

When confronted by a defensive person, allowing them to vent while you listen is best. A knee-jerk reaction would be to defend yourself. If you intervene too quickly by justifying your behavior, the person will become more defensive. Connect with the person by listening reflectively, asking exploratory questions, and recognizing and validating their feelings. Doing so takes the wind out of their sails, knowing you are trying to understand them rather than defending yourself.

In our leadership workshops and coaching sessions, we often role-play situations where we assume the role of a problematic coachee, such as being aggressive or highly passive. In the leader's attempt to coach us, they often exhibit several common and ineffective coaching snafus. The following describes the top five challenges of a leader-coach.

Ask Rather Than Tell

Many leaders tend to explain the problem before asking the direct report for their perspective. For example, a coach might say, "In the past month, your performance has been subpar," when they could have said, "In the past month, how would you rate your overall performance?" Asking allows the communication door to remain open to create a collaborative conversation.

Address the Emotions First

If you do not address the person's emotions first, you will have a difficult time connecting with the individual. Why? Because of how the brain works. Emotions are stored in the primitive brain, the limbic system. The prefrontal cortex part of the brain contains our logical and rational thoughts. When we experience emotions, the limbic system is activated, and the logical part of the brain slows down. The stronger the emotional reaction, the higher the chance of becoming stuck or emotionally hijacked in the primitive brain. At that point, logic and rational thoughts diminish, leading to poor decisions.

For example, you might say to an angry person, "You appear pretty upset about this." (Pause and wait for a response.)

"You bet I am," they reply.

"What is causing you to be so upset?"

"Well, I have been working with you for . . ."

The person's emotional energy around their responses dictates how you should respond. When they react less defensively, their logical brain is more active and ready to have a logical conversation.

Recognize and Validate People's Feelings

When someone shares how upset they were over an incident, it is not uncommon for coaches to nod their heads and softly reference something like, "I understand." This alone is not an empathic statement. To display empathy, you must recognize and validate a person's feelings. Try something like, "You appear pretty upset about this," or "I would also be upset if this happened to me." An automatic disconnect occurs when a coach fails to recognize and validate a coachee's feelings. The bond of all relationships is formed while validating individuals' feelings.

Several years ago, I, Keith, was asked to deliver a half-day workshop to a first-tier supplier in the auto industry on the topic of "Adjusting to the Stress of Change." During lunch, the VP informed me that he needed to share some new information with the employees before my workshop.

Minutes before I was about to speak, the VP informed the employees that due to financial challenges, they would now be personally responsible for paying 20 percent of their healthcare costs.

After that bombshell announcement, he answered a few brief questions, handed the microphone to me, and exited the room.

I was just as shocked as everyone else and could not escape the feeling that I had just been ambushed. There I stood, looking at a mob of angry workers wanting to take my head off! As the facilitator for the class, I was the easiest of targets. As I listened to them vent, I quickly recognized how we could apply today's workshop to what they just experienced. But first, I had to deal with the collective anger over what they had just heard and assure them that I was not a plant working with the company.

After listening for thirty minutes, I was able to help them reframe their situation with the thought, "Although you cannot change this inevitable event, you can control the way you deal with it." We took a quick break, returned with renewed focus, and shifted our attention to the content of the workshop I was scheduled to present.

Identify and Address Body and Nonverbal Language

During a coaching session, a person might roll their eyes, fold their arms, or slouch in the chair with a disgusted look. What would you do? Many leaders/coaches struggle with nonverbal communication. They continue telling the coachee their perception of the direct report's poor performance. Like two ships passing in the night, they are disconnected from one another due to the leader's inability to respond to body language.

The study of body language dates to the work of Darwin's *The Expression of the Emotions in Man and Animals*, published in 1872. *Body language* was popularized in the 1950s when Professor Albert Mehrabian of UCLA found the 7–38–55 percent rule when communicating.[2] He theorized that 7 percent of communication is words, 38 percent includes tone of voice, and 55 percent is body language. Professionals jumped on the bandwagon, helping the public recognize the importance of body language. Over the years, scientists studied the importance of body language, questioning Dr. Mehrabian's 7–38–55 percent rule. Some research supports that body language accounts for 60–80 percent of communication.[3] Regardless of the percentages, most agree that body language and nonverbal messages are critical in communication. Words are important and convey essential information, whereas body language reflects attitude and emotions.

It is critical to point out that although there is good science regarding body language, it is an area that has led to poor, unsubstantiated information and often remains subjective on the viewer's part. For example, saying that someone who folded their arms is defensive or closed off can be erroneous. Maybe they are cold or feel more comfortable sitting in a chair with folded arms due to the chair's ergonomics. Body language experts know not to interpret one movement but rather a cluster of body gestures and movements. Remarkably, many leaders remain blind to the body language of their direct reports, leading to communication breakdowns and interpersonal disconnect.

Manage Angry and Aggressive Behavior

Nothing is more challenging for a leader/coach than managing someone who becomes unglued during the coaching session or vents vehemently and verbally attacks the coach. Although this tends to happen to a varied degree, when it does, it can send many coaches into a defensive tailspin.

When confronted by an angry person, remain calm. One mistake we often see is the coach engaging in verbal combat with the coachee. This will surely escalate the confrontation. A more effective approach is seen in how professional hockey officials handled players fighting in the 1950s and '60s compared to officials today. Back in the day, officials attempted to break up the fights immediately, only to find themselves taking a pounding. Today, officials stand back, and only when players become exhausted do officials move in and separate them. The same should be done in the coaching session.

Since the coachee has pent-up emotional energy, allow them to vent while you listen reflectively. As you remain calm and listen, they will often talk themselves down from their emotionally hijacked position. You can then recognize and validate their feelings, which will then allow you to converse logically.

When coachees become angry and aggressive, the 4-R tips can help you break through resistance:

- **Recognize and validate feelings:** "It appears you are upset about . . . How is this affecting you?"

- **Reveal beliefs:** "What challenges are you experiencing? How do you think it will affect you?"

- **Reframe distorted beliefs:** "That's interesting. I see it a little differently." (The coachee will most likely respond by asking, "How do you see it?") You can then offer, "I wonder what alternative ways of looking at this might be helpful."

- **Reinforce their beliefs:** "How do you see your role?"
  "What are the potential advantages of X?"

STEP 4: CREATE THE PLAN

You can now mutually agree on goals and create an action plan to solve the problems or issues discussed. This includes identifying steps to be taken, what will be done, and a timeline. An action plan establishes a level of accountability and understanding between you and your direct report. An action plan template could look like this:

1. Determine the skill area to develop.
2. Establish the learning goal (must be specific and behavioral).
3. Determine what knowledge and resources are needed to achieve the goal.
4. Identify the action steps necessary to reach the goal (training, classes, books, videos, etc.).
5. Agree upon a timeline for achieving the goal.
6. Establish checkpoints and agree upon follow-up.

STEP 5: CLOSE THE MEETING

Now that your goals and plans have been identified and agreed upon, it is time to bring the meeting to a close. Be sure to summarize the meeting by bringing out the highlights discussed. Ask your direct report how they feel about the process and if they have any questions or need clarification.

This is also the time when you discuss the follow-up process. Following up is critical to the success of the coaching process. Be sure to explain the process and engage them in the discussion. Then, agree on the checkpoint dates and times of the follow-up meetings. The meeting can be formal or informal depending on how the person is performing. Unfortunately, many leaders take the time needed for steps one through four but fail to take the necessary time to follow up.

There are two main reasons why following up is so important. First, if the coachee is executing and accomplishing the identified goals, you want to recognize those achievements. Or, if they're not following through with the plan's goals, you need to address the inaction. Set up a meeting to discuss your concerns, identify reasons for the lack of execution, and then support the person to succeed.

Insights

Your direct reports want . . .

- consistent and ongoing coaching and development.
- to be coached to self-discovery, not to be told what to do.
- to explore and find more profound nuggets of their behavior—*peel the onion.*
- a collaborative process and plan to help them grow.

CHAPTER 11

Build Trust

She has favorites and doesn't trust anyone, fostering a hostile and jealous work environment between coworkers.

Have you ever felt the sting of being burned by someone you trusted? Perhaps they were close friends or family members. Or maybe the connection was more distant, and you were on the receiving end of an online scam. Take a moment and think about how you felt when this happened. What were those feelings? They could include hurt, anger, or vulnerability. Regardless of how close or distant the connection might be, experiencing the break of a trust bond can be emotionally devastating. Trust is the foundation upon which relationships are built and the glue that bonds all relationships, professional and personal.

The work of Paul Zak, the founding director of the Center for Neuroeconomics Studies and professor at Clairmont Graduate

University, yielded some interesting statistics regarding trust in his article titled "The Neuroscience of Trust."[1]

Statistics show that for people at high-trust companies:

- 74 percent are less stressed
- 50 percent are more productive
- 13 percent take fewer sick days
- 76 percent are more engaged
- 40 percent show fewer symptoms of burnout

However, one unanswered question for years has been why we trust some people and not others. Is it something learned, or is it innate?

New Science on Trust

Research has taught us that people are hardwired to trust one another. However, there are times when we know that we should be cautious about a particular person. Our instinct to trust often makes us vulnerable to various scams or unethical sales tactics that find ways to infiltrate our areas of vulnerability.

Is there more going on in the brain that signals us to be vigilant? Thanks to neuroscience research, we better understand the need to trust and connect with others, even when we feel we should be on guard. Thanks to Zak's work, it's been found that there is a neurologic signal that tells us when we should trust someone. He found that ". . . having a sense of purpose [see Chapter 15] stimulates oxytocin production, as does trust. Trust and purpose then mutually reinforce each other, providing a mechanism for extended oxytocin."[2] Yes, the *love drug* our body naturally produces is a hormone that promotes positive feelings and empathy, like endorphins and other neurotransmitters.

To further test the effects of oxytocin and trust, Zak conducted an experiment that showed a similar result. Using a synthetic oxytocin via a nasal spray, he administered one group with that nasal spray and another group with a placebo. The group receiving the oxytocin doubled the amount of money given to a stranger compared to the placebo group. He also found that this group did not demonstrate unusual behavioral risk. "Oxytocin appeared to do just one thing—reduce the fear of trusting a stranger."

We Live Up to the Level of Trust Given to Us

Regardless of what many argue, people tend to live up to the amount of trust given to them. This is one of the human behavior truisms we presented in Chapter 3.

Take, for example, the Miller's Bar in Dearborn, Michigan. Since 1941, they have served the number one–rated burger in Michigan. However, this restaurant is unique because customers do not receive a bill at the end of their meal and are instead asked to rely on the honor system. The customer tells the cashier what they ate, and then they pay. While you might think this would be a money-losing proposition, the opposite effect has occurred, and this restaurant continues to flourish.

So, what makes Miller's Bar so successful? Are the burgers that much better than those from the restaurant down the street? Some might say they are good but not necessarily the best burger in metro Detroit. However, what adds to the success of this restaurant is the trusted relationship they have created between themselves and the customers. By treating customers with respect, honesty, and, most importantly, trust, the payback is that of a satisfied returning customer and loyalty.

Think of this analogy regarding your direct reports. How trusting are you of their daily activities in managing and accomplishing their work? Assume for a moment you took the Miller's Bar approach and trusted your direct reports implicitly (just as Miller's does with each table bill). Imagine how loyal they would be to you and the organization.

In another example, we purchased some items at the gift shop when training at a large conference center and hotel. When we went to pay, there was not a cashier. Instead, there was only a price list and a cash box. We smiled and looked around for a camera. Although we saw none, we still did the right thing and paid. Upon leaving the following day, we asked the desk manager if the cash box was ever short. He laughed and said that most of the time, there was extra!

Again, we share these illustrations with a caveat. We believe most people are ethical and trustworthy (brain science tells us so); however, a small percentage of people are unethical and corrupt. As a result of this small percentage, we have many societal laws and policies in the workplace. So, it comes down to a balance between trusting people and being cautious and safe. Trust but verify.

To further illustrate this point, some time ago, a woman came to Keith seeking counseling because she caught her husband in an extramarital affair. After months of counseling, the couple was able to repair their marriage. Over the next few years, the wife would check in to report how they were doing. In one of our conversations, she explained that she was suffering from what she termed *justifiable paranoia.* Not being a term found in our psychological dictionary, he asked what she meant. She explained that when her husband told her he would be home at 7:00 p.m. and instead arrived at 8:30 p.m., she became very suspicious. This woman's reality is not unlike what many people experience today. A little skepticism is understandable in a world of unscrupulous behavior, such as on the internet or in our daily lives and compounded by our inherent need to trust.

The System Is the Problem

The problem many organizations face today is that they have created an environment of distrust. When you consider the policies, procedures, and behaviors found in the workplace, it is not surprising that a *Harvard Business Review* survey found that 58 percent of people said they trusted *strangers* more than their boss.[3]

As leaders, we are often on the front lines of either reinforcing trust with our direct reports or creating an ongoing wedge. Consider the numerous forms of distrust found in most organizations today. If a direct report is sick, some must bring a doctor's note to back up their claim. Rather than trusting direct reports, we use time clocks to provide calculated accountability. We even install security systems to ensure people are working and not slacking off.

In a recent webinar that we created on managing a remote workforce, the number one issue on leaders' minds was, "How do I know my direct reports are being productive and actually working while at home?" However, as one leader concluded, the nature of this question only tells you the level of trust that exists between that leader and their team.

In his article titled "Alan Mulally's Management Secret: Peer Accountability," healthcare leader Rod Collins shared a story from Ford Motor Company highlighting the importance of building trust.[4] Back in 2006, Ford hired Allan Mulally as their new CEO. For several years, their company had been in decline, and they needed someone who was going to come in and turn things around. Initially, Mulally's presence was met with resistance by some on the team. They didn't like Mulally's approach to leadership and, in particular, his weekly Business Plan Review (BPR) meetings.

One of the primary objectors to this was a long-time Ford executive, Mark Fields. When he was just thirty-six years of age, Fields had run Argentina's Ford operations and became the CEO of Mazda (then owned by Ford) at age thirty-eight. He was on a meteoric rise and undoubtedly felt he had strong credentials to eventually take over the CEO position at Ford. But that did not happen, and his frustration showed. Because he assumed the newly hired Mulally would view him as a threat and seek to challenge or push him out of the company, Fields decided to bring things to a head quickly. At their weekly leadership meetings, each leader was asked to bring a color-coded chart representing their department's performance in their assigned areas. Green meant on or above target, yellow was average, and red meant efficiency was off schedule. Fields brought his chart and marked it all red. The room grew tense.

Rather than being angered at this apparent disrespect, Mulally saw this as a teaching moment and used it to help the team see his leadership perspective. This was a valuable lesson in leadership transparency exhibited by one of Mulally's senior leaders. From there, Mulally and Fields developed a friendship, and in 2014, when Mulally retired, Fields succeeded him and held the CEO role until his retirement in 2017. Mulally saw the negative culture established at Ford as a more significant threat than one man's display of resentment. And as a result, he was able to be a strong catalyst for change.

Why People Lack Trust

If leadership is more about the relationships created, then trust is a cornerstone of leadership. Trust is not just something you say; it's something you do. A relationship is built as two people get to know each other. The more you know about a person, the easier it is to trust or mistrust them. This is a gradual process that takes time to develop. Initially, you might share more of yourself and extend some of your trust to others. From there, you can gauge how they respond. Do they embrace this new level of trust or abuse it?

This relationship is seen in all aspects of life, whether you are asking someone out on a date or confronting a friend. It is why many avoid conflict or sharing troubling information with their boss. Opening up and being emotionally vulnerable is the critical thought underlying one's willingness to share information to build trust. Yet, when parties respond with support and acceptance, trust prevails and strengthens the relationship.

Trust is broken when promises are dismissed, and commitments are not kept. It happens when someone drops the ball and doesn't follow through, betraying our confidence.

Trust is broken when any of the following occurs:

- Interests become self-serving
- Excuses are offered in place of taking responsibility
- Credit is taken for other people's work
- One thing is said while another is done
- Favoritism of other direct reports is on full display
- Temperaments are uneven and unpredictable
- Difficult decisions are sidestepped
- Poor performance by favored team players is overlooked
- Assumptions are made without checking the facts
- Direct reports do not have a chance to explain themselves
- Micromanagement becomes the default, while delegation is an afterthought

The following analogy by Stephen Covey makes a good deal of sense. People make bank deposits and save money, and when they need that money later, they withdraw it. Leaders can create a metaphoric emotional bank account with their direct reports. But instead of money, trust is used. After many deposits by the leaders, the person feels safe when it's time to take some out.

Stephen Covey, in his best-selling book *7 Habits of Highly Effective People*, identifies six ways to make deposits (or reduce withdrawals):

1. **Understanding the individual.** This means listening intently to what the other person is saying and empathizing

with how they may feel. It's essential to care for others and act with kindness toward them.

2. **Keeping commitments.** How do you feel when someone arrives on time when you have a meeting? How about when people do what they say they will do? You build up an emotional reserve by keeping your commitments.

3. **Clarifying expectations.** We are not mind readers, yet we consistently expect others to know what we expect of them. Communicating our expectations can help create a higher level of trust. When we ask for what we want and get it, we can trust a little more.

4. **Attending to the little things.** Don't you find that the little things tend to become the BIG things when they do not receive our attention? Doing the little things is how we honor and show respect for others.

5. **Showing personal integrity.** Integrity is the moral foundation upon which trusting relationships are built. When we operate with sound moral character, it makes it so easy for others to trust us.

6. **Apologizing when we make a withdrawal.** We will make mistakes; it's part of life. But when you see you have violated trust, sincerely apologizing is how we make a deposit to counteract the damage we have done.[5]

Our most precious relationships (with our significant other, kids, friends, and boss) require constant deposits because those relationships continue to grow and change, and with these changes come new expectations.

Make the First Move

Ultimately, trust can only be established when someone makes the first move to develop it. It is incumbent upon leaders to make the first move with their coworkers. This can become risky since the coworker has not proven or demonstrated their trustworthiness. Leaders must first build a trusting environment within an organization, team, or department. This can only happen when they have accurately assessed the level of trust in their organization.

You can understand the trust level among your team by examining some basic analytics or observations. For example, what is the turnover rate in your organization? Chronic rumors, finger-pointing, turf protection, and we/they attitudes are visible behaviors associated with signs of low trust.

If you want to understand your direct reports' perspectives, in your next team meeting, ask your direct reports to anonymously rank the level of trust in your team, department, and you on a scale of 1–100.

Warning: You may be in for an eye-awakening surprise; it takes courage to collect this information. Our survey reveals that 35 percent of respondents said their leaders were not trustworthy. We guess the number is higher since 60 percent said they would fire their boss. The percentages would increase if we added numerous reasons why they thought their boss should be fired. For example, *does not provide open and honest feedback* (31 percent), *does not act with integrity* (25 percent), and *does not delegate* (14 percent), are all critical elements of trust.

Depending on what research or surveys on trust you read, you will find that upward of 70 percent of direct reports mistrust their leaders. According to the Edelman 2020 Trust Barometer, 57 percent do not trust their leaders.[6] Regardless of what you read, mistrust in leadership remains a critical challenge in corporate America.

Build Trust Through Delegation

Trust is enhanced when leaders delegate. Although it's not at the top of our survey list of reasons people would fire their boss, 14 percent said they would do so because of the lack of delegation. With leaders doing more with fewer resources, delegating is critical. Yet, many leaders struggle in this area. In fact, delegation is often rated poorly in many inventories used to assess leadership strengths. Why do leaders struggle with delegation? Indeed, it is an easily understood skill yet challenging to execute.

There are several reasons why leaders struggle. First, delegation is often seen as a binary issue—delegate or don't delegate. A binary perspective decreases the options when a leader contemplates whether to delegate an important project. What appears to be a simplistic decision for leaders may, in fact, require them to consider other possibilities.

Second, some leaders tend to have perfectionistic or controlling tendencies. "I can do it better than others." All the while, they rob themselves and their teams of the benefits of handing off projects to their direct reports, who can grow into roles and exceed the current standard of excellence. This, of course, brings us back to the issue of lack of trust. It is hard for leaders to believe in others to do high-quality work. Often this stems from a previous time when they handed off a project and the results were disastrous.

Finally, there is the challenge of time. Many leaders feel that coaching and mentoring take too long to gain traction. However, effective delegation becomes an essential skill for leaders when used as a tool to develop a person, team, trust, and relationships.

However, when delegation is approached improperly, it can demotivate others. This is heard with comments like, "Why me? I have enough on my plate," "I always have to do it," or "It's their responsibility, not mine." If this is what you typically hear, it is a sure sign that how you delegate needs some improvement.

THREE COMPONENTS OF DELEGATION

There are three components of effective delegation. The first is *what*, the second is *to whom*, and the third is the process of *monitoring and follow-up*.

The *what* refers to identifying the actual project or tasks to be delegated. It requires an analysis of the project. Questions to ask yourself would include: What skills are needed? What are this project's goals, objectives, and other requirements?

The *to whom* refers to a specific person. Effective delegation requires assigning projects to people best suited to complete their tasks. We must ensure they have the necessary skills and insight to succeed. Other things to discuss include why they were chosen, the expected results, checkpoints and deadlines, and where their responsibilities begin and end. Keep in mind that you should avoid delegating to the same person repeatedly. As a leader, one of your goals should always be to be as inclusive as possible.

This brings us to *monitoring and follow-up*. Regardless of how well you accomplished the first two parts of the process, do not hand off the project and walk away thinking all will be well. It is imperative to take time to monitor the project without falling into the trap of micromanagement. Check in to see how the person you have assigned is progressing. This allows time to correct mistakes, check for possible stress levels, and offer ongoing feedback.

Flawless execution rarely happens, and there will be times when you will need to regroup and ask some exploratory questions. Explain your concerns and inquire about what they did or didn't do. Together, explore the reasons for the disconnect. Was it a resource issue, miscommunication, or other possibilities? Did someone else tell the delegate to do it differently? Then, collaboratively search for solutions.

Building a RICH Trustworthy Environment

Trustworthy relationships do not happen overnight, and the RICH acronym is helpful. This provides you with four keys to follow.

Reliable and Respectable: People who work with you need to know they can count on you. This means you must be available, accessible, and demonstrate predictability and consistency. It's doing what you say you will do and understanding each other's working styles.

Integrity and Intimacy: Create a safe and secure environment where people openly share things with you. Maintain a positive mindset while demonstrating positive regard for others. Let go of grudges and know your direct reports on a personal level.

Communicate and Be Credible: Consistently share accurate information, communicate as a calm adult, and listen and inquire. Be more upfront with information and "walk the talk."

Humble and Honest: Be more other-centric as opposed to being self-centric. Get your ego out of the way and meet the needs of your direct reports (not your needs). Demonstrate an open, honest, and genuine concern for others.

- Admit your own mistakes

- Give credit where credit is due

- Take time to apologize

What Happens If Trust Is Broken?

Sometimes, trust can be broken to such a degree that it is almost beyond repair.

To rebuild trust, your thought process needs to be challenged by:

- Maintaining integrity

- Disputing negative, unrealistic thoughts

- Recognizing that the past does not always predict the present or the future

- Evaluating the event, situation, and people involved from a current perspective, not the past

- Recognizing that being cautious does not indicate mistrust

Inspiring trust means being trustworthy and demonstrating behaviors that give people confidence in you and show others that you have confidence and trust in them.

Insights

Your direct reports want . . .

- to be thoroughly trusted.
- more professional and personal information about you.
- you to delegate more.
- you to consistently demonstrate RICH behaviors.

CHAPTER 12

Motivate and Appreciate

*I wish he would be more involved in
my day-to-day work so he has a better
understanding of what I actually do. I feel
like most of the time, I'm on my own.*

One of the most misunderstood concepts in business is motivation. Yet, it is also one of the leader's most essential skills in their toolbox. The problem is that many have been taught incorrectly. Hundreds of speakers have spent millions on the motivational speaking circuit for decades. However, the hidden secret that so many attendees of these seminars should know is that you can't motivate someone!

For example, remember in high school or college when you took your Introduction to Psychology class. You might recall reading

B. F. Skinner's work in behavioral psychology that started in the 1950s. More specifically, Skinner's method of learning, what he called *operant conditioning*, states that when reinforcement follows a behavior, that behavior is likely to repeat itself.[1] This is illustrated in breakthrough experiments when pigeons and rats learned to peck the lever and were reinforced with food. Skinner also introduced the concept of negative reinforcement. In his Skinner's Experiment Box, the box floor contained an electric grid. Skinner would turn on the grid, sending a shock to the rat. Eventually, the rat learned to push a lever to stop the shock. Hence, the beginning of reward and punishment.

Konrad Adenauer, the first Chancellor of the German Republic, once said, "I reserve the right to be smarter today than yesterday."[2] This is well stated in how behavioral psychology has grown over the decades. Nothing is more evident than understanding motivation. While we can condition lower-functioning animals to jump, find food, and peck all day for a reward, it is a different story for humans.

While humans might be more conditioned by food when they are starving, motivation takes on a very different meaning when they are not lacking these basic needs. When understanding motivation, people and organizations suffer from what Gestalt therapist Karl Duncker termed *functional fixedness*.[3] This is defined as a cognitive and psychological bias that limits a person to seeing any object or issue only in the way it has traditionally been used or seen.[4] To illustrate this point, we replicate a classic Duncker experiment in our classroom settings. It goes like this.

Using only a candle, a box of thumbtacks, matches, tape, and scissors, attach the candle to the wall so that wax does not drip onto the floor when the candle is lit.

If you tried pinning the candle to the wall with a tack or melting part of it and sticking the candle to the wall, it did not work—functional fixedness. The solution is to empty the thumbtacks from the box, attach the box to the wall with a thumbtack, then melt some wax from the bottom of the candle and stand it upright in the box before lighting it. Surprising as it might seem, most people struggle to find the correct solution.

This revelation prompted Duncker to tweak the experiment with one minor change. Removing the tacks from the box, he quickly discovered that most individuals successfully solved the problem. Simply changing one detail reduced their functional fixedness and got them to *think outside the box*.

The results from Duncker's experiment are clear: People often have a functional fixedness bias. That said, consider how many leaders continue to hold antiquated beliefs to motivate, reward, or punish people. We see this play out in organizations and society often.

The Contrast Between Rewards and Punishment

Organizations began to adopt behavioral psychology and applied many principles to managing people. One of these most popular principles is the carrot and the stick: If you do *this*, you will get *that*. The belief is that if rewards and punishment work well with other *animals*, it will be an excellent way to motivate *humans*. But does it?

According to Alfie Kohn, author of *Punished by Rewards*, if a leader's goal is to effectively change a person's behavior in the long term, rewarding or punishing them is ineffective.[5] Do rewards and punishment motivate people? All of this depends on the type of motivation used and the types of individuals who make up the population. But a simple answer is yes. As Kohn asserts, it motivates people to get rewards. In other words, the person focuses on attaining the reward instead of the work itself. Conversely, when punished, the person's goal is to develop creative ways to avoid punishment.

To clarify this point and demonstrate the difference between punishment and rewards, we often do an exciting and fun activity in the classroom. Two volunteers are selected and sent out of the room. When this happens, the class must devise a primary task they want these two volunteers to perform. Generally, this is something as simple as touching the flipchart. Neither volunteer knows what they are supposed to do.

When the first volunteer attempts to figure out the task and continues to fail, they receive a punishment. For example, a leader is instructed to gently tap them with a light foam noodle when they move away from the desired task. It's often not long before the volunteer runs around the room attempting to escape the impending *punishment*.

Contrast this with the next participant. In their attempt to figure out the task, they receive positive reinforcement. Every time they move closer to the desired task, the class cheers and claps louder, which serves as a *reward*.

This simple illustration drives home this fundamental truth: People who are punished focus on avoiding punishment, whereas people who receive positive reinforcement direct their attention to figuring out how to complete the task.

Two Types of Motivation

Let's explore motivation on two different levels. *Intrinsic* motivation is when you engage in a behavior because you find it internally rewarding. It's working at company X because of their values and culture. Engaging in behavior because you are rewarded is an example of *extrinsic* motivation. I work at ABC company because they pay well, and the benefits are good. The research is clear: Intrinsic motivation is more powerful than extrinsic motivation in changing behavior in the long term. Therefore, if your goal as a leader is to create conditions for high performance, quality, and cooperation, then focus on the intrinsic motivators and use the extrinsic motivators sparingly.

In psychology, there is a phenomenon called the *overjustification effect*. "Overjustification occurs when extrinsic rewards (such as money and prizes) are given for actions that people already find intrinsically rewarding; therefore, the person becomes less internally motivated to pursue those activities in the future."[6] Unfortunately, we find this plays out far too often in organizations.

Growing up and working in the Detroit area, we have spent many years providing our services to the automotive industry. On one of these occasions, while speaking about the importance of motivation in the workplace, Tony, a frontline worker, offered some pushback. He stated that his paycheck was the only reason he came to work and that his "brothers and sisters should be making a lot more money."

Tony lamented that he and his frontline workers did not receive more perks and benefits than those in management. He pointed out that this had become a typical conversation among disgruntled employees on the team. And from this interaction, we had a conversation that went like this.

> Keith: "You probably do deserve more pay."
> Tony: "You better believe it."
> Keith: "Tony, do you like your work here?"
> Tony: "It's OK, but it can get a little boring sometimes."
> Keith: "I imagine it can. I'm curious: Do you have any hobbies?"
> Tony: "Yeah, I like working on my old car on the weekends."
> Keith: "I bet you're good at it. And you spend a good deal of time over the weekends working on your car because you enjoy it?"
> Tony: "I love it."
> Keith: "But you don't make any money doing it."

At this point, Tony laughed and replied, "Yes, but I love it." He obviously got the point. Many workers work at uninteresting and monotonous jobs, leaving some intrinsically deprived. As a result, workers become hyper-focused on external things to fill the void.[7] In Tony's case and thousands of other workers, the immediate extrinsic reward provides a short-term solution. But as time passes, so does gratification, and soon, the cries of "we want more" are heard. There will always be jobs people do not enjoy. The critical point is tapping into a worker's intrinsic needs and desires. When leaders recognize this importance, they can create ways to make the job more acceptable.

Compensation May Not Be an Effective Motivator

The importance of compensation has been studied and debated over the past decades. In her 2005 book, *The 7 Hidden Reasons Employees Leave*, Leigh Branham revealed that 89 percent of bosses believe employees quit because they want more money.[8] As much as any boss would wish this statistic to be accurate, it is not. Only 12 percent of employees leave an organization for more money. As John Maxwell notes, "People quit people, not companies."[9]

In the 1940s, there was a well-regarded psychologist named Fred Herzberg. His Two-Factor model has been adopted and applied by numerous organizations worldwide. Herzberg identified two sets of factors related to understanding motivation in the workplace. Some factors lead to employee satisfaction and motivation. The other leads to dissatisfaction and unhappiness.[10] Herzberg was adamant that a person's salary is *not* a motivator. As mentioned earlier, extrinsic motivators have a short lifespan. It is what we call *the red car theory*. If I only had that red car, I would be happy! People always want more. To be sure, people want to be paid a fair wage and will compare their pay to others.[11]

One could argue the merits of Herzberg's theory because some people are motivated by money. Take a starving, homeless individual, for instance. Cash in hand takes precedence over their need for recognition and status. But, like most human issues, everything is situational. A more significant question is, does money motivate people to higher performance? Kohn would argue it does not. Consider the following: In your department meeting, you announce to your direct reports that starting June 1 through the end of August, they must work every weekend. However, there is no need to worry because the company has agreed to pay them time and a half. That would go over like a lead balloon. Do you believe people will arrive at work on Sunday morning with an *I'm so happy to be here* attitude? You would get people to come to work, but with a mindless obedient attitude they would do what they have to do: perform at a low level.

One final story regarding pay and motivation.

Our CPA once called us for some advice. He wanted to recognize his direct reports' hard work in the past tax season. Since the summer is traditionally a slow time, he wanted to offer Fridays off to the entire staff and pay them for the day: a thoughtful and generous gesture. We asked him why he felt he needed to pay the staff for a day off. He replied how upset they would be if they were not paid. We disagreed and tried to persuade him that the intrinsic value of long summer weekends is worth more than the extra dollars. He disagreed, and a lunch bet was wagered. A few weeks later, the response was overwhelming. No one complained about not being paid for Friday. He offered people the option of working Friday with pay, but only a few did, and most took Fridays off. Needless to say, we enjoyed a delicious lunch!

How to Motivate Others

How do you motivate others? Here is a secret—you can't. Motivation is an internal process that is different for each person. What motivates Tina is different from what motivates Fred. What leaders can do is create motivating conditions for people to be successful.[12] Personal success breeds motivation. Remove the success and people feel demotivated.

Therefore, the first two steps for leaders to create a motivating climate are:

1. Get to know them personally.

2. Modify or remove the demotivators.

Our survey showed, for example, that only 40 percent of leaders took time to learn the personal aspects of their direct reports' lives. For the remaining 60 percent, the challenge of creating the necessary successes exists. Second, consider the demotivators in your organization's policies or culture. Does a direct report need to bring in a doctor's note if they are ill for more than three days? Are the direct report's bags searched when leaving the premises? Are you tracking their arrival or departure times via a badge or computer log in? These are some of the numerous examples that lead to demotivation.

Returning to Herzberg's research, he identified several factors that influence motivation. At the top of the list is the need for direct reports to be recognized for their efforts and successes. Sadly, our survey found that nearly 50 percent of the respondents reported their leaders failed to recognize their work. According to the O. C. Tanner Institute, their survey found that 79 percent of workers quit their jobs due to a lack of appreciation![13]

Think about the thousands of workers across America who feel unappreciated and not recognized by their leaders who are walking out your doors. It is not difficult to understand why a talent war is occurring. Yet, much of that could change by simply communicating praise, approval, compliments, and saying thank you. To create successful opportunities for a direct report, emphasize intrinsic motivators and take time to know those who report to you. Acknowledge their efforts and utilize Kohn's three Cs—collaboration, choices, and content. Direct reports work well and feel motivated when they collaborate, have choices, and produce meaningful content (their work).

While *collaboration* is often listed as a leadership competency, it is not always practiced. For many leaders, it is easier to tell people what to do rather than take the time to collaborate. However, you must involve others in a collaborative process to create a more motivating climate that engenders creative solutions, engagement, and commitment. Remember, people do not like to be told what to do.

Choices give people a sense of autonomy, which is a need for all workers. This leads to an increase in intrinsic motivation. Tell Jackie she needs to work on Project X, and she will do it. Ask if she prefers to work on Project X, Y, or Z, and she will select the most rewarding one.

Content relates to the actual work the direct reports do each day. The level of intrinsic motivation increases when a person's work is seen as interesting and meaningful. As Herzberg notes, "If you want people to do a good job, give them a good job to do."[14]

Insights

Your direct reports want . . .

- you to create successful opportunities so they feel a sense of motivation.

- you to understand them and what is important to and for them.

- more opportunities to experience intrinsic motivators.

CHAPTER 13

Inclusion and Belonging

*Too many times, I feel as if my
ideas are not being heard.*

In today's environment, an organization's focus and emphasis on advancing its capabilities around diversity, equity, and inclusion has never been more critical. Boards, corporate executives, managers, and employees are often asked to hold each other and themselves to a much higher standard in the workplace. Organizations that invest efforts into inclusion and belonging do so for heartfelt reasons. Often, businesses recognize this renewed focus as being the right thing to do.

As a leader in the workplace, please don't misinterpret the right thing to do as insincerity or being politically correct. A company must operate on a set of core values and beliefs, and there is a moral and ethical obligation to ensure employees and leaders are held to such standards.

In addition, the success of companies is rooted in employees being valued and feeling a sense of belonging. As leaders, your goal should be to harness your direct reports' varied talents, backgrounds, and experiences.

Intuitively, we know that diversity and inclusion matter. However, it also makes good business sense. A recent study by the international consulting firm McKinsey found that companies in the top quarter for gender, racial, and ethnic diversity are likelier to have financial returns above their national industry medians. Conversely, companies in the bottom quartile in these dimensions are statistically less likely to achieve above-average returns. It's fair to conclude that diversity is a competitive differentiator, shifting market share toward more diverse companies over time.[1]

Equality vs. Equity

There is much misunderstanding regarding what diversity and inclusion is and what it is not. A common misconception is that focusing on diversity means *special treatment* for certain groups of people. If this is what people think diversity and inclusion mean, it is easy to understand the confusion or resistance toward these efforts.

One of the most significant distinctions in making this point all the clearer is understanding the differences between *equality* and *equity*. At first, these two terms look very similar. They sound very similar as well. However, they are very different. Equality is defined as treating individuals similarly, regardless of needs and requirements. Equity, on the other hand, is defined as constantly and consistently recognizing and redistributing power. These two definitions and concepts can often challenge our very paradigm of how we think. Since we were young, we have been taught the importance of fairness and equality. Most of us who are parents or even children growing up with siblings have been raised with the concept of sharing equally.

An analogy to consider is the visual picture of three individuals attempting to look over a concrete wall to view an event occurring on the other side. Each of these individuals ranges in height, with a child at 4 feet, a woman at 5 feet, and a man at 6 feet 8 inches. However, to be equal, they are all provided with the same step stool to stand on and look over the wall. From an *equality* standpoint, the image on the left shows everyone with the same size step stool. However, this doesn't necessarily help those who are shorter than others. On the other hand, when we think of the situation with *equity* in mind, we look to give everyone what they need to be successful—to see over the wall. It may not mean giving everyone the same thing, the same size step stool. Giving everyone the same thing, assuming it will make everyone equal, creates the assumption that everyone started at the same place.

Diversity and inclusion are not about special treatment but rather about increasing your organization's capacity to identify and embrace employees' ideas, opinions, talents, innovations, and creativity. When leaders embrace a diverse mindset, it helps employees feel valued while driving the business bottom line with out-of-the-box thinking.

EQUALITY   EQUITY

Source: Interaction Institute for Social Change | Artist: Angus Maguire

Creating an Inclusive Workforce

The engagement levels of an organization are directly impacted by the extent to which all talent is intentionally included in the day-to-day contributions of the workforce. This requires separate definitions of the terms diversity and inclusion. Diversity includes those qualities and characteristics that make us unique or different. Diversity is measured by workforce composition, perhaps at various organizational levels. The presence of diversity by nature can create conflict, which, when well-managed, creates innovation. Inclusion is simply the *act* of including. It is not a state of mind or an environment. However, when combined with the intention to drive contribution, the impact of inclusion is increased engagement levels within the organization.

One of the most concerning blind spots that leaders face is creating an inclusive workforce. This blind spot often occurs for a variety of reasons. As leaders, you are constantly under pressure to deliver. You deal with projects, deadlines, fires to fight, etc., and as a result, leaders often have go-to direct reports. These are individuals you have trusted time and time again. They come through for you, make your jobs more manageable, and ensure the project will get done. Once these people have been anointed, you begin to establish those *in the house* and those *out of the house.* When people are *in the house*, they are *in the know* and get the preferred projects and assignments.

This begs the question: How does this happen? How do we get to this point, subconsciously creating our go-to people who are *in the house* and those looking from the *outside in*? Often, this is established by the very essence of inclusion or lack thereof.

As a leader, ask yourself how often you have had a meeting after the meeting. You may have had a conversation in the hallway where you shared additional information with an individual in the meeting. Or you invited some of your favorite people to lunch while leaving others at the office. Perhaps you have found yourself resorting to grade school–like practices, sitting with your best buds at lunch in the cafeteria.

Another example could be that you discover one of your direct reports, Joe, is a good golfer, like yourself, so you invite Joe to go golfing. In doing so, you fail to check with others in the office to see if they would like to come along. You may have an unconscious bias for why you didn't extend the invitation to others on the team. Maybe you assumed that some team members don't play solely based on a lack of discussion of a weekend golf game or a belief that someone may have a spousal or child commitment.

Regardless, the lack of inclusion is critical in leading to the unintended building of those actions. Even in a casual golf outing, relationships are formed, trust is established, and projects or work assignments may informally be discussed. Leaders must become ever more conscious of the implications that inclusion or, in this case, lack of inclusion has in the workplace.

Whether we admit it or not, we often spend time with those with whom we share things, such as common interests, values, and experiences. Whether it's the university we attended, the church we are associated with, or the school our kids attend. All of this begins to feed into the essence of inclusion or lack thereof. However, by always relying on the default of those go-to direct reports, we limit the ability to seek different perspectives, specifically those that may differ from our point of view.

It's important to remember that inclusive leaders help organizations attract the best available talent. This is crucial because it results in more high-quality talent for your business and brings insights and experiences from underrepresented customer groups. This can help shed light on problems that more homogenous teams have been stuck on and are unable to resolve.

According to the Gartner Research Group, examples to help remove where the most common blind spots exist around inclusiveness for leaders include:

- Share the credit
- Explore ideas without dismissing them
- Listen and ask questions
- Recognize excellent work

- Provide additional context on urgent requests

- Allow for more autonomy and decision-making

- Honor one-on-one meetings with direct reports

- Provide regular, constructive, informal feedback

- Take an authentic interest in well-being and career goals[2]

An Example of the Power of Inclusion

IDEO, a design and consulting firm founded in Palo Alto, California, is an excellent example of an organization that embraces inclusion, innovation, and creativity. IDEO's culture comprises a flat hierarchy emphasizing autonomy, creativity, and collaboration. They have been responsible for inventing such products as Apple's first mouse. However, the real genius within IDEO is the diverse and inclusive talent engaged in projects. Rather than a primary team of design engineers, IDEO has a diverse employee base with employees who have backgrounds in science, the arts, music, and many other areas.

About twenty years ago, ABC's *Nightline* produced a segment about a challenge given to the IDEO team to completely redesign shopping carts in less than a week.[3] Within just a few days, they created a more functional cart than many previous competitors who had been around for years.

The belief that companies like IDEO share is that it is not the leader who has the best ideas. Instead, there is a need for an enlightened trial-and-error method that sees the product from the eyes of the consumer. The entire team feels valued because their contributions are recognized as meaningful.

Going back to our survey, one of the things we asked those who took the survey to do was select the reasons why they would fire their supervisor or manager. Twenty-nine percent said they would do so because their leaders did not value diverse thoughts and opinions. Similarly, a study from DDI found that 69 percent of employees believe their leaders do not promote an inclusive environment.[4]

Why is this the case? Two main reasons: biases and ego.

A Peacock Named Perry

We use an animated story in our Diversity and Inclusion course called *A Peacock in the Land of Penguins*.[5] In this story, a colorful peacock named Perry becomes an employee in a company in the penguins' land. The senior team was comprised of all penguins dressed in their tuxedo-type garb. The employees in the company were other species of birds, such as robins and doves, and they all looked and behaved differently from the company's leaders (the penguins). The story's theme is how Perry, a peacock, and his friends were excluded from the business operations and how difficult it was for the penguins to accept differences.

Spoiler alert! When wolves infiltrated the penguins' land (a corporate takeover), Perry and friends spotted the wolves and collaborated with the penguins to prevent the wolves from taking over. This nail-biter ending reveals the importance of diversity, inclusion, and biases.

Looking at your organization, is there a relationship between the Land of Penguins and your company? Is most of your senior leadership team made up of penguins? People who look and think alike? Who are the peacocks and other birds, and how are they treated?

An organization's culture does not develop randomly. It is created by top leaders who bring their vision, ideas, and opinions of how they see the company functioning and offer their feedback. This is not a bad thing. The company's values and philosophies can benefit the company and its employees. The challenge is being aware of and effectively managing our innate need to surround ourselves with like-minded people. By doing so, consciously or unconsciously, we tend to exclude people who are different from us. In other words, biases come into play.

Three Types of Biases

Unconscious biases are thoughts and feelings that happen unconsciously in the brain, creating quick judgments and assessments of people and situations, which are influenced by our background, cultural environment, and personal experiences. Since all people are biased in some way, it becomes essential for leaders to recognize how their biases influence their decisions. Then, they must make a conscientious effort to overcome these limiting beliefs.

Three types of biases shape our perspectives: *affinity* bias, *confirmation* bias, and *perception* bias.

AFFINITY BIAS

Affinity bias favors people who are like us. Picture two candidates with similar credentials, skills, and motivation to do the job well. However, one graduated from the same university as you, majored in the same program you majored in, and was in the same sorority. The other candidate graduated from a different university. Who would you select?

CONFIRMATION BIAS

Confirmation bias is the tendency for people to seek information that supports or confirms their point of view, beliefs, or assumptions. For example, perhaps you have always been concerned about diversity issues in America. As a result, when a new inclusion and belonging committee is formed at your workplace, you decide to join the committee. You believed this issue was necessary, and when someone else agreed with your belief, you were immediately hooked.

PERCEPTION BIAS

Perception bias is the tendency to form stereotypes and assumptions which make it impossible to make objective judgments. In Keith's dating years, a friend of a friend fixed him up with a relative from a small town in Ohio. Their conversation covered typical first-date topics such as sports, politics, family, and religion. Something strange and interesting happened once she learned Keith was from the Jewish faith. Throughout the remainder of the dinner, she kept looking at his head. As Keith became more self-conscious, he asked her why she kept looking at his head. She responded by inquiring where his horns were located and if it was true that they fell off when he turned thirteen.

This was undoubtedly a stereotype Keith hadn't been aware of about those of the Jewish faith having horns.

Five Ways We Can Combat Unconscious Biases

There are several ways we can combat unconscious biases. First, recognize that all people have biases, even yourself. Do some self-examination and evaluate your attitudes toward diversity. Next, identify where and when these biases surface. What situations, mental images, or media portrayals cause your bias meter to go through the roof?

Third, accept their existence as being a learned or conditioned process. And from this acceptance, embrace new ideas, opinions, and feelings of others. Focus on utilizing everyone's unique talents and strengths. Fourth, consciously and firmly challenge this bias and the beliefs that come with it. Remember, your direct reports are always watching what you do. Hold yourself accountable to them, and as you grow in this area, provide opportunities for those on your team to learn and be mentored in this area.

Finally, replace the old belief with a new accepting belief. Recognize that leadership is all about relationships. Promote collaboration and continuously keep your unconscious biases and other blockers in check.

Insights

Your direct reports want . . .

- to be accepted and included.
- you to leverage their uniqueness and individuality.
- you to become aware of and combat your biases.

CHAPTER 14

The Pursuit of Well-Being

They continue to dump more work on us—
can't they see the stress we're under?

Here is a classic joke among psychologists.

A new patient arrives for his appointment in the late afternoon, with bandages on both ears. The doctor immediately asks him what happened. The patient explains, "I overslept and had to get to the office for an important meeting. I jumped out of bed, took a quick shower, took my suit out of the closet, and saw that the pants were wrinkled. I ran into the kitchen, started the coffee, got the ironing board, started ironing my pants, and then turned on the news. As I watched the news, ironing my pants and drinking my coffee, the telephone rang . . . With the iron in hand, I mistakenly put the iron up to my right ear and quickly said hello."

Trying to maintain emotional composure, the doctor says he understands how the patient's right ear got burned, but then asks what happened to the fellow's left ear.

The patient responds, "I had to call an ambulance."

Stress and Burnout

While this story may be just a joke, it points to a larger truth: how the level of stressed-out workers continues to increase, impacting the loss of productivity, performance, and engagement.

According to the APA's Work and Well-being Survey (2021) of 1,501 of adults:[1]

- 79 percent of employees experienced work-related stress in the month before the survey.

- Three in five employees reported negative impacts of work-related stress. This included being disengaged and having low energy and motivation.

- 36 percent reported cognitive weariness.

- 32 percent were emotionally exhausted.

- 44 percent reported physical fatigue.

When stress is not effectively managed, it can lead to a person *burning out*. According to the World Health Organization, burn-out is characterized by exhaustion, negativism or cynicism related to their jobs, and disengagement from work.[2] It's been reported that the number one reason for burnout is the nature and volume of one's workload.[3]

These statistics are concerning. Step back and ask yourself, are we more stressed out today than our parents, grandparents, or great-grandparents? Many argue that we are. We believe that with the pace of change that comes with technology and global competition, our society and workplace are experiencing VUCA times. VUCA is an acronym for Volatility, Uncertainty, Complexity, and Ambiguity. The acronym was first used after the collapse of Soviet Union in 1991. The US Army War College used the term to describe how leaders must be more strategic in challenging times.[4]

Considering the preceding statistics and data, mental health problems, a disengaged workforce, and employees experiencing a high level of stress continue to flood organizations. Companies can no longer place blame on individuals or superficially address this epidemic. The time has come for organizations to provide workers with a psychologically safe workplace.

The Stress from Change

Like all changes, there will be resistance and negative consequences. Why? When change occurs, it affects everyone in an organization. It is essential to point out that it is not the change, per se, that causes people to experience stress. Instead, it is the transition, a psychological process of moving from the old habitual behavior to a new set of behaviors, that produces frustration, anger, and anxiety in people.[5] Just think about any habit you attempted or changed. For example, think about your emotional state of mind when you try to quit smoking or lose weight. It's a challenge due to the tidal wave of emotions.

Combine this psychological transitional process with what neuroscience has revealed: Our brain perceives change as a threat and will always take the path of least resistance in dealing with it. The brain likes predictability and always looks for the low-hanging fruit to resolve a challenge or problem. If it is too difficult, it will look for what is easiest and what it knows (old habits). When this happens, we define this as a person's *resistance* to change. They continue to do the same things the same way, hoping for a different outcome, also known as Einstein's definition of insanity.

Change Is a Transitional Process

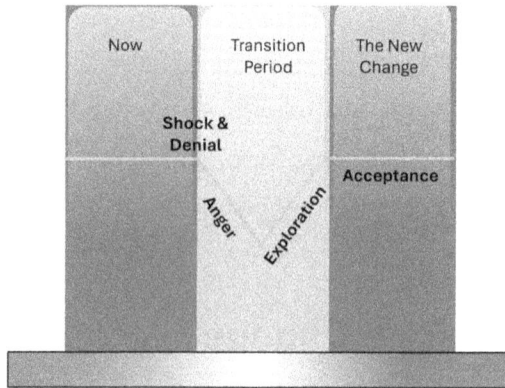

Employee Engagement and Stress

Employee engagement has been a significant concern for organizations across the US for the past several years. Although there has been a slight increase since 2022, disengaged employees remain a primary concern for leaders. In our quest to better understand the relationship between employee engagement, stress, and one's overall well-being, we discovered some interesting connections.

It is always interesting how we enjoy categorizing or placing labels when a significant change occurs—for example, the term *quiet quitters* has infiltrated the workplace. Quiet quitters give minimum effort and are psychologically disconnected from work. There is even a term for the worker who is disconnected and undermines a company's goals: *loud quitters.*

Gallup has found that most employees are quiet quitters. They discovered that 59 percent are quiet quitters, and 18 percent are loud quitters, leaving only 23 percent of people thriving at work. Because of these quitters, it is estimated that the global economy loses about $8.8 trillion per year.[5] You can see why employee engagement, or the lack thereof, remains a critical issue facing organizations.

But is there a relationship between the level of stress and the employee's engagement? Intuitively, we say there would be. After all, if a worker is dissatisfied with their work and workload, frustrated with their manager, and stressed out due to long hours, one could surmise this person will become just another disenchanted, mindless, obedient body at the workplace.

It appears that Gallup's analysis agrees with our intuition. They found that 44 percent of employees experienced great stress the day before taking the survey. In other words, low engagement is related to higher stress levels. We agree that it's not just low engagement at work that influences one's stress. If you factor in issues like financial concerns, relationship problems, aging parents, and other familial challenges, employee stress these days remains at an all-time high.

What Organizations and Leaders Can Do

Many employees spend more time at work than they do with their families. The workplace offers a structured environment where workers socialize, form meaningful relationships, and are integrated into people's self-worth and self-esteem. Besides the transactional work and tasks employees are responsible for, organizations and leaders can no longer avoid the human needs that exist in every employee.

Senior leaders can argue that they provide their employees with paid time off for vacation or personal time, fair compensation, and other perks and benefits. We agree, but is that enough? When you consider the number of disengaged workers burned out and leaving their jobs for greener pastures, organizations and leaders must do more.

The workplace landscape has changed since the COVID-19 pandemic. The mental health crisis sheds light on the needs of employees and the importance of what organizations and leaders need to do to remain competitive.

During our research for this book, we compiled a comprehensive list of actions that organizations and leaders can take to enhance the support and resources provided to their employees. Based on the abundance of research in this field, we categorized the list into six areas: Workload, Autonomy, Involvement, Recognition, Training, and Purpose.

WORKLOAD

Workers today are over capacity due to limited resources, job demands, and deadlines. The amount and nature of their work creates a lot of stress for employees across the US. Combined with endless meetings (as one of my coachees said, "We have meetings to discuss meetings") and the plethora of emails, texts, chats, etc., blowing up their computers, by the end of the day, workers are exhausted, only to experience additional stressors at home.

In the 1980s, Francesco Cirillo invented a time management method called the Pomodoro Technique. It uses a timer to break work into intervals, twenty-five minutes in length, and separated by a short five-minute break. It has proven useful in many organizations, providing workers with increased accountability and motivation and decreasing mental fatigue and stress.[6]

It appears that Cirillo's technique had some validity. However, it has become evident that the Pomodoro method is not suitable for all industries. If we were in critical condition in an emergency room, we would not want the medical staff to take a five-minute break when the timer goes off. Nevertheless, this technique has advantages and encourages organizations and workers to reconsider their work hours. We can find proof of this in nature and sports. For instance, migrating birds fly in a V formation to increase efficiency and reduce energy consumption. Similarly, hockey teams employ four lines (groups of players on ice), with each line taking turns skating hard for around 45 seconds before the next line replaces them. This rotation continues throughout the game.

Suggestions for improving workloads:

- Identify creative ways to help your employees pace their work.

- Find ways to reduce the number of meetings.

- Create calendar blocks to build in private time and time free of meetings.

- Prioritize emails.

- Learn to say no, as opposed to saying yes only to regret it every time you are faced with something you don't want to do.

AUTONOMY

Two of our *human-behavior truisms* state that people do not like to be told what to do, and that people prefer choices. For decades, behavioral scientists have shown the importance of employees working their best and being less stressed when they have flexibility and feel a sense of control over their work. Yet, organizations and senior leaders continue to deprive employees of this inherent need for human beings.

Suggestions for increasing worker autonomy:

- Provide flextime, time off, childcare, and other services that allow more choices and flexibility for employees.

- Allow employees to create work schedules.

- Provide options for where, when, and how employees work. Every worker is different; there is not one shoe that fits all employees. For example, some workers enjoy working from home, while others prefer working at the office.

INVOLVEMENT

Per the Gallup Survey cited earlier,[7] employee engagement has 3.8 times as much influence on employee stress as work location. Employees who find their work engaging and inspiring tend to be happier and more productive. Social interaction is vital for people, and work can provide this opportunity. If the hybrid work model remains the new norm for workers, finding ways for workers to connect socially becomes even more important. For many people, it can become habitual to remain sequestered in their homes. Be sure to find time during and after work to engage with your team. By being actively involved in their work, employees develop a sense of camaraderie and mutual support, leading to a community where everyone has each other's back.

Suggestions for getting workers more involved:

- Remember, people learn to make decisions by making decisions. Get them involved in the decision-making process.
- Continue to solicit feedback.
- Move from giving orders to giving intent.
- Continue to provide positive support.

RECOGNITION

It is a natural human desire to be acknowledged, valued, and appreciated. Recognition is an important protective factor against stress and burnout, as stated by the *Monitor on Psychology*.[8] Recognition is often related to job performance, but appreciation is more about the individual's worth and perceived value. Both recognition and appreciation are crucial for all employees. Unfortunately, many leaders fail to recognize this reality.

Suggestions for increasing recognition of employees:

- Although financial recognition like bonuses can motivate many, offer more intrinsically important things like praise and other social rewards.

- Send a private note or publicly recognize the person.

- Give gift cards.

- Always look for ways to bolster a person's self-esteem.

TRAINING

At our company, we offer leadership training to organizations of all sizes. We are constantly surprised by the number of untrained leaders we come across. As discussed in previous chapters, leaders are often promoted for their technical abilities, but being a truly insightful leader requires an entirely separate set of skills.

Providing professional development for supervisors, managers, and leaders is crucial, as they are directly engaged with employees. This includes improving their core leadership skills and teaching them how to support their direct reports.

Although many companies offer an Employee Assistance Program, services like mental health and addiction counseling, educational services for children, and other resources, employees struggle to connect with these services for various reasons.[9] Sadly, this puts them at risk despite the availability of such programs.

According to Michael Schultz, co-founder of Aclaimant, a risk management company, "The risk is omnipresent, but there has never been a more important issue facing today's workplace than the risk associated with an employee's ability to access qualified mental health services. With an insight-driven workflow and advanced analytics RMIS system, we are witnessing an increased demand to replace the traditional Employee Assistance Plan with an interactive, analytics-driven mobile device option that can enable everyone to become a risk manager. Better, Safer People is no longer an option."[10]

Suggestions for beefing up leadership training:

- Promote mental health awareness.

- Encourage work-life harmony.

- Add inclusion and belonging training.

- Create a psychologically healthy culture by treating people empathetically, fairly, and with respect and dignity.

- Reevaluate company policies and procedures to include mental health provisions.

PURPOSE AND VALUES

The next chapter focuses on the employee's purpose, meaning, and authenticity. But we wanted to point out here that purpose and values can either advance or hinder one's career path and are directly associated with stress and burnout. Many employees struggle with conflicting values between themselves and their company, leading to frustration and a sense of meaninglessness.

We were introduced to a senior engineer via a referral from his company. The company was recently acquired by an organization outside of the United States and was a union facility with around three thousand employees. This engineer had a friendly and positive working relationship with the frontline workers, often engaging in activities such as bowling and golfing with them. However, the new senior leaders at the company offered him a promotion to the vice president of the engineering department on one condition: He must cease all socializing with the frontline workers. Feeling conflicted, he sought our guidance.

After speaking with him, it became clear that traditional coaching methods could not solve his dilemma. Instead, it was a matter of conflicting values. On the one hand, the VP position was a desirable advancement for which he had worked hard. On the other hand, he believed that successful and insightful leaders should maintain positive relationships with all employees. We advised him to take some time to consider his options deeply and to contact us if he needed further assistance. Two weeks later, he resigned, and the company lost a talented engineer.

Suggestions for supporting worker purpose (and values):

- Take time to reflect and recognize what it is about your work that inspires and motivates you.

- Take a moment to reflect on what aspects are lacking in your work and what steps can be taken to improve them.

- If you are feeling stressed, try to identify the specific source of your stress. Is it related to an issue between you and your manager, organizational problems, or a conflict with your role?

The Rx Factor: Team Leadership

In our survey, many respondents discussed the emotional state of their leaders. Words like *grumpy*, *negative attitude*, *frustrated*, and *stressed-out* were often found in the over four hundred written responses, indicating that leaders are struggling to manage their own stress levels. As we previously mentioned, emotions are contagious, and leaders need to take the advice of flight attendants and put the oxygen mask on themselves before helping others. If leaders are unhappy, irritable, and worried, they will spread the stress virus to their teams. Therefore, it is crucial to manage one's stinking thinking.

If stress is defined as the body's response to change, leaders must prioritize keeping their immune systems strong. Managing your stress and emotions and considering how they affect your mood and behavior is essential. It's also important to ask yourself how others perceive you.

After managing your emotions, checking in on your direct reports is crucial. Insightful leaders must know their direct reports beyond their skills and knowledge base. They must understand their motivations, passions, and values. Recognizing employees as individuals with unique qualities and contributions is essential. One respondent in our survey said, "I wish my boss would treat me as a person, not a number!"

The more you know your direct reports, the easier it is to recognize their struggles. You will notice it in their behavior, language, and attitude. If you suspect someone is struggling, don't wait. Meet with them, share your concerns, and offer support. Even if you misread the situation, acknowledging your concern and empathizing is always beneficial.

We are reminded of a story a supervisor shared in the class-room when he worked on the floor in an auto plant. An employee with a reputation as a good worker but who struggled with self-criticism, which often led to sadness, was transferred to his department. With this in mind, the supervisor consistently gave him positive feedback and built him back up when the worker was down. One Friday morning, he noticed the worker looking a bit distressed and was about to leave his office to connect with the worker. Before leaving the office, the supervisor was alerted to an emergency on the other side of the plant that required immediate attention. Consequently, he did not have an opportunity to talk with the worker. On Monday morning, the supervisor learned that the employee died by suicide. As the tears rolled down the supervisor's face, we took a break from class, and we helped him reframe the unfortunate situation.

Hopefully, you will never experience such a tragedy. Remember what best-selling author Simon Sinek eloquently said, "Your role as a leader is not about taking charge but taking care of those in your charge."[11]

To maintain a healthier body and mind, incorporate simple tips like taking a ten- to fifteen-minute power nap, enjoying a peaceful lunch away from your computer, consuming nutritious and ener-gizing foods, moving your body regularly, and disconnecting from technology at a reasonable time to spend quality time with friends and family. Sleeping seven to eight hours is crucial for a more robust immune system. Remember, as a leader, taking care of yourself and your team's well-being is paramount.

Insights

Your direct reports want you to . . .

- build a solid social support system, professionally and personally.

- keep the door of communication open with friends and colleagues.

- maintain unshakable optimism during tough times.

- spread positive feelings.

- maintain hope: **h**ave **o**ptimal **p**ositive **e**motions.

- reframe your stinking thinking.

- view life as challenging but with opportunity.

CHAPTER 15

Meaning, Purpose, and Authenticity

My manager is the most phony and insincere person I know!

The German philosopher Friedrich Nietzsche is known for saying, "He who has a why to live can bear almost any how." One wonders how much of an impact Nietzsche's statement had on the work of the renowned thought leader today, Simon Sinek, in his best-selling book *Start with Why* and the works of psychiatrist Viktor Frankl, *Man's Search for Meaning*.

Frankl's ideas, philosophy, and his development of logotherapy resulted from being a prisoner in Auschwitz and other Nazi concentration camps during WWII. Nietzsche's quote is found throughout Frankl's book and appears to be the foundation upon which many of his hypotheses are based. Although Frankl's work resulted from his imprisonment and the horrific atrocities he experienced, his explanation and understanding of how and why many prisoners chose to live instead of giving up their will to live is immeasurable.

In the foreword of *Man's Search for Meaning*, psychologist Gordon Allport wrote that Frankl stated, "What alone remains is the last of human freedoms—the ability to choose one's attitude in a given set of circumstances."[1] Further in the book, Frankl writes, "Man, however, is able to live and even die for the sake of his ideals and values."[2] Nietzsche, Allport, and Frankl agree that a person's meaning of life, ideals, and values form their beliefs and interpretation of how to best deal with any situation.

Frankl also reports on a survey taken by 7,948 students and 48 colleges throughout the US and conducted by Johns Hopkins University. While the year of this survey is unknown, we assume it was in the late 1950s to early 1960s. The survey asked what students considered very important to them. Sixteen percent said money, which makes sense for any college student. However, 78 percent said, "Finding purpose and meaning to my life."[3]

Later in life, Frankl applied his theory of logotherapy in his psychotherapy practice. He defines logotherapy as the "striving to find meaning in one's life as the primary motivational force in man."[4] Yet, as Frankl espoused, and many today agree, countless people are challenged with finding their true meaning in life; they are caught up in a situation that Frankl defines as an *existential vacuum* (what we call being *hollow*).[5]

We believe many people are stuck in this existential vacuum or living a hollow life. In their quest for immediate extrinsic things (which many have been conditioned to want), such as money, power, toys, etc., they develop hollow ideals, values, and beliefs. They have become blinded to what is important: to live a more authentic and genuine life. Think about the multimillionaire who experiences a life-threatening health diagnosis. A common thought is how they would give up their money to regain their health. Sometimes, it takes adversity for people to regain insight into what is truly important.

Research from the aftermath of the COVID-19 pandemic continues to pour in. Workers around the US began to reflect and rethink their work and personal lives. Approximately forty-seven million workers quit their jobs in search of work that provided more time with their families, flexible hours, and was more aligned with their passions.[6]

This Great Resignation is far from over.[7] The hardship of the pandemic was costly psychologically and financially. Yet with significant changes, some positives did emerge. Workers reimagined their lives by moving away from the conditioned mindset of "I live to work" to "I work to live." Workers again are searching for how their work provides meaning to their lives.

More recently, Simon Sinek's book, *Start with Why: How Great Leaders Inspire Everyone to Take Action*, discusses the importance of the "Golden Circle," which explains why leaders and organizations do what they do.[8] Surely all companies understand what they do and how they do it. For example, we can tell you what our company does: provide professional development and executive coaching to large, medium, and small companies internationally. We do this by delivering world-class courseware virtually or in a classroom setting. But it is *why* we do what we do that inspires and motivates us to get up each morning. Our *why* is to help organizations create an environment that empowers employees and instills pride and satisfaction in their workers. We want to help companies build a more human-centric culture resulting in improved employee satisfaction, productivity, and effectiveness.

Think about it: Every organization knows what and how. However, as Sinek points out, only some people, leaders, or companies can clearly articulate why they do what they do. When a person's why, how, and what are in balance, authenticity is achieved. When out of balance, people become confused and uncertain about the true meaning of their work; they're stuck in the existential vacuum.

Authenticity

We often say in the classroom that for leaders, theory is important, but it's the skills and behaviors that can be modified and strengthened that will make the difference. When educating leaders on nebulous concepts like trust, social-emotional intelligence, and authenticity, it is often challenging to define them clearly enough for the desired behaviors to become evident.

Living authentically means being true to yourself and holding a moral compass that aligns with genuine values, purpose, passion, and honesty. This has been a way of life widely accepted by most people and highly valued for decades in America. However, over the past two decades, things have changed. From the emergence of divisive and ugly politics to being scammed by phone and emails and even manipulated by AI, people are now more than ever seeking authenticity. While some consistently try to fake it, their inauthenticity leads to inner turmoil and unhappiness. But as Dr. Grant Hilary Brenner eloquently asked, "You can counterfeit a Picasso, but can you counterfeit yourself?"[9] As previously mentioned, it's common for people to search for and reflect on living a more authentic life.

To keep things simple and not get bogged down in theory, our model will help you better understand the facets of authenticity.

Cognitive Authenticity + Behavioral Authenticity = Interpersonal Authenticity

Cognitive Authenticity (the way you think) includes the following abilities:

- To consistently introspect and reflect
- To assess your strengths and weaknesses
- To be self- and socially aware of your thoughts and feelings
- To elicit opinions, ideas, and feedback from others

Behavioral Authenticity (the way you act) includes the following abilities:

- To be accountable and not shift blame onto others
- To be other-centric, humble, and treat people with respect and dignity
- To communicate transparently
- To demonstrate trustworthy behaviors

Cognitive Authenticity, together with Behavioral Authenticity, leads to Interpersonal Authenticity, which creates:

- Genuine connection with people
- Trusting relationships and teams

- An enhanced level of empathy
- Inspiration in yourself and others

Having a Purpose Is Healthy

Indeed, meaningful work is motivational and leads to higher performance and satisfaction.[10] But does having a purposeful life affect your health? Intuitively, if one has meaning and lives their values and beliefs, they are most likely more satisfied and happier. It appears the research supports our intuition. Kilian Abellaneda-Pérez found that a stronger sense of purpose in life promotes cognitive resilience.[11] *Cognitive resilience* refers to the brain's ability to manage stress and other injuries, thereby reducing the risk of significant symptoms or disabilities.

Our intuition regarding the importance of meaningful work grew over the years after reading the inspirational author and speaker Zig Ziglar's book *See You at the Top*. His infamous quote, "Your attitude determines your altitude,"[12] resonated strongly. With that quote in mind, we asked participants in several of our workshops, "Bottom line, what are you looking for out of life?" Philosophical sounding? Yes, but it is not that profound based on the typical four answers we hear after asking thousands of leaders and individual contributors this question. Although we hear many different responses, most fall into one of the four categories, as seen in the following image.

Regardless of where employees sit on the organizational chart, everyone states they want to be in the positive cycle. We have never met someone who claimed they want to live in the negative cycle. Unfortunately, as seen in other chapters of the book, far too many people struggle to live an authentic and meaningful life, leaving them stuck in the negative cycle.

Leader's Attitude

Authentic
Meaningful
Work

Happy

+

More Productive
Engaged

Positive Energy
Motivated

Inauthentic
Meaningless
Work

Unhappy

–

Feelings are contagious

Unproductive
Disengaged

Negative Energy
Unmotivated

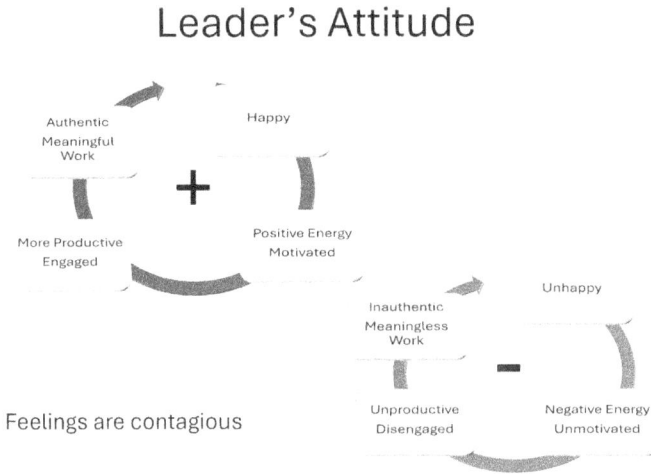

Still not convinced? Boston University School of Public Health researchers found that people with higher levels of purpose may have a lower risk of death from any cause. That association is applicable across race/ethnicity and gender. And if you're not wowed yet, consider what Surgeon General Dr. Vivek Murthy recently stated: "Loneliness poses risks as deadly as smoking fifteen cigarettes a day."[13] After reading these statistics, our curiosity led us to investigate further to understand the seriousness of the loneliness factor.

As social creatures, we recognize the importance of our need for interpersonal interaction and connection. But why does the surgeon general refer to this as an epidemic? Part of the reason is that the COVID-19 pandemic brought to light several issues and problems not seen pre-pandemic. Examples include the mental health issues discussed previously, as well as the changes in workplace structure. When COVID-19 fell upon the world, organizations operated completely virtually, and many eventually created a hybrid work model. People socially isolated themselves. Employees conducted business out of their homes and on their computers. Our need for social connection was unmet.

The following metaphor can provide a better understanding of the consequences of our social needs going unmet. Built within our brain is a social thermostat, like the thermostat in your home to regulate room temperature. Similarly, our social interactions influence the balance of our social thermostats. When our need was not met during the pandemic, for example, our thermostat became imbalanced. Our desire increased but was not attainable, leaving us frustrated and unhappy. This is akin to being on a diet and wanting a piece of the double chocolate cake you cannot have. You become internally conflicted, leading to a higher level of stress.[14] Depending on the person and frequency of being socially out of balance, it can result in a mental health problem.

The pandemic appears to have exacerbated the loneliness epidemic. Over the past two decades, social disconnection among friends and family members has increased.[15] With the advent of technology, social media, and the internet, many people are left feeling alone in our densely populated country.

Since employees work about forty-eight hours a week, the workplace is a natural environment for friendship and social interaction. Even though the pandemic contributed to social deprivation, there are ways to create and maintain friendships at work. One of the courses we virtually provided was Managing Remotely. Many leaders were creative in their attempt to keep their teams connected. *Send in a baby picture and let's figure out who the person is*, or *Take a picture of your home office and let's try to identify the person* were two creative activities. The cocktail hour suggestion was unique. After a virtual work meeting, people remained online to chat about anything but work as they sipped their favorite beverage. One team met in the office's parking lot, circled up in their cars, and rolled down their windows to chat.

Research has certainly brought to light a better understanding of the importance of social interaction within society. From the workplace to families, "Having social connections is one of the most reliable predictors of a long, healthy, and satisfying life."[16]

What Leaders Can Do

Employees find that meaningful work is "more important than any other aspect of work, including pay and rewards, promotion opportunities, or working conditions."[17] How a person defines meaningful work is determined by the individual and has various meanings. In other words, no one or two factors increase or decrease a person's sense of purpose. Unfortunately, the feeling that one's work is meaningless persists for many employees. Leaders and an organization's culture cannot make an employee's work meaningful, and existing behaviors and systems can quickly damage an employee's meaningfulness. Authors Catherine Bailey and Adrian Madden identified five qualities of meaningful work.[18] Based on our experience, we took the liberty of modifying and expand the five qualities to eight.

OTHER-CENTRIC

Other-centric thinking focuses on how work transcends itself to other people. It's about how other-centric leaders focus on what they do or don't do that affects the people they lead. In contrast, narcissistic, self-centric leaders remain focused on their accomplishments and achievements. It's been found that humble leaders (other-centric) receive increased commitment, trust, creativity, engagement, and job satisfaction from the people they lead.[19]

> **LEADERS TIP:** Positively focus on what your direct reports do regarding their roles and performance.

PASSIONATE

When workers discussed what made their work meaningful, it was far more than happy events. People recall difficult and even painful times that led to meaningful moments. When the General Motors Willow Run Facility closed, we were called in to help employees deal with the stress and change workers experienced. When having lunch with a foreman on the line, he discussed how the years of working with good people and contributing to a fine product made him feel worthwhile. Although he was not looking forward to moving to Arlington, Texas, to resume his work as a foreman, he believed he could make a difference for other workers.

> **LEADERS TIP:** Help your direct reports find their passion by discussing their jobs' good and challenging elements. Explore ways to increase their curiosity about the work they do.

EMOTIVE

Meaningfulness was not the result of a series of frequent and ongoing events. Instead, it occurred when people recalled a significant emotional event that triggered a sense of meaning in their actions. Emotional events like surviving a heart attack or losing a loved one can create a new meaning for a person.

> **LEADERS TIP:** Ask if they ever had an experience, good or bad, that led to a significant learning moment, and then discuss it.

SELF-AWARENESS

As discussed earlier, workers today are doing more work with fewer resources. From ongoing meetings to performing their tasks, most people need to take time to introspect and reflect on what is important to them, professionally and personally. Therefore, any sense of meaningfulness remains unconscious. Only when you become more aware of your thoughts, feelings, and behavior can you consciously experience something.

> **LEADERS TIP:** Take the time to explore with your direct reports how they approached a given process that led to a successful or unsuccessful outcome. Also, help them express whatever feelings they may be experiencing related to the event.

WORK-LIFE HARMONY

The work-life balancing act is an old paradigm that does not hold for workers today. It suggests that work and personal life are separate entities that must be balanced. Work-life balance focuses on keeping your work and personal life separate but equal. In contrast, work-life harmony is centered on the belief that there is no distinction between the two and that both must coexist.[20] This has been found when workers experience their work as meaningful, not as a separate entity but as an integration between their professional and personal lives.

> **LEADERS TIP:** Know your direct reports, including their goals, values, beliefs, and as much personal information as they are willing to divulge.

PRIDE AND ACHIEVEMENT

Workers who take pride in their work often feel a sense of meaning. We spent many years at Detroit Deisel Corporation when Roger Penske bought the company. We trained their leaders and non-leaders for many years. A fellow named George was the custodian who oversaw keeping the training center clean. Although he could have made more money working in the plant, he chose the lower-paying job of maintaining the training center. Without fail, every day we arrived at the training center, George, with a smile from ear to ear, asked us how the floors looked. He cleaned and waxed the floor like an early recruit in the military would shine their shoes.

> **LEADERS TIP:** Find time to recognize people's achievements no matter how inconsequential they may be for you.

PRAISE AND APPRECIATE

Given that our newest research shows that 60 percent of workers would fire their boss, there were more than four hundred comments about why they would fire them. Numerous explanations included the need for recognition and never feeling appreciated or acknowledged by their boss.

A 2020 white paper by O. C. Tanner Learning Group titled *Performance: Accelerated* found that:[21]

- 79 percent of employees who quit their jobs claim that a lack of appreciation was a significant reason for leaving.

- 65 percent of Americans claimed they weren't even recognized one time last year.

It's a simple concept to understand, yet many leaders remain blind to this critical element of making work meaningful.

> **LEADERS TIP:** Find opportunities to acknowledge, recognize, and provide positive feedback to your direct reports.

COLLEGIAL ENVIRONMENT

As previously mentioned, meaningfulness is an internal process that each person determines based on the eight elements and numerous other factors. However, the feeling of meaninglessness results from external factors, like poor leadership or a highly bureaucratic organization whose only focus is on the bottom line, contributing to employees' disengagement. In past chapters, we discussed the importance of creating an adult environment where leaders create thinkers motivated to share their intentions, leading to a collegial discussion. Unfortunately, too many leaders continue to lead with a carrot and stick, only to reinforce a direct report's feelings of meaninglessness.

> **LEADERS TIP:** Create a team of adults by acting as a colleague. Ask instead of tell, listen for understanding, and recognize and validate feelings. Remember, your direct reports are always watching you.

Employees who find their work meaningful tend to be happier, more satisfied, and healthier than those who don't find meaning in their work. Unfortunately, there are many leaders and organizations that remain blind to these facts and continue to create meaningless conditions for workers. The way out of this existential vacuum is to explore and find your why.

Insights

Your direct reports want you to . . .

- help them find and understand their *why*.
- be authentic and genuine.
- live and breathe the eight qualities of meaningful work.

CHAPTER 16

Attracting and Retaining Talent

It's like a revolving door around here.
Good people are always leaving.

Matt remembers a conversation he had with one of the business leaders he had supported at a previous organization.

The leader walked into my office and looked utterly shell-shocked. I could see on his face that he was at a loss for words. I asked, "Jack, you look like you saw a ghost; what happened?" He said he was just stunned by the worst business news he had in a long time, and to make it even worse, the news took him by complete surprise. I asked him what had occurred, and he said, "My best employee just turned in their resignation, and I never saw it coming."

> I hear this story time and time again. Leaders are blind-sided by the resignation of a cherished employee—yet another example of a leadership blind spot.

This scenario has played repeatedly way too often. Imagine you're a manager, sitting in your office, and everything is going well. Then, one of your top employees approaches you and asks if you have a moment. As those fateful words come out that they are resigning, numerous thoughts go through your mind. You realize they are a critical player in your team's success, and you are losing them. They have been well trained, formed strong relationships with your customers, and understand the business. In fact, this person never complained or even took much of your time.

At this point, what can you do? What are your natural reactions or responses to the employee? "We can match whatever pay you're getting," "I'm sure I can get you that promotion we have been talking about . . ." and "What will it take to keep you?" Or lastly, and most desperately, the infamous, "Pleeeeeaaase, don't go!" While we may make many statements in desperation, the reality is that it is too late to save an employee once they have resigned.

A Battle for Talent

For many years, we as a nation have chosen to declare *war* on various topics. Going back ninety years, Franklin Roosevelt, in his presidential inauguration speech in 1933, declared war on the Great Depression. In addition, we have seen the war on drugs, crime, capitalism, and now, to no surprise, a war on talent! The current landscape of talent retention in businesses is constantly evolving, with lack of employee engagement, quiet quitting, and turnover all escalating issues that all managers are grappling with. It's essential that as a manager, you not only focus on retaining talent but also excel at keeping the talent engaged and satisfied.

Throughout this chapter, we will explore the cost of turnover, why employees are choosing to leave, what strategies you can take to help mitigate this turnover epidemic, and further explore which employees (quiet quitters) have decided to leave the organization but continue to arrive every morning to work and continue to get a paycheck.

The Cost of Turnover

In today's highly competitive business environment, the war on talent continues to intensify. Talent is the lifeblood of any organization, and retaining this talent is crucial for long-term success. High staff turnover is costly, not only in financial terms but also in terms of lost productivity, morale, and institutional knowledge. The war is won by those who effectively manage their talent, leveraging strategies that prioritize talent retention and mitigate the negative effects of quiet quitting. Before we can appreciate and accept the cost of turnover, let's first begin by breaking down the different types of turnover: planned vs. unplanned.

Planned turnover is most often within the manager's control. For example, retirements, job eliminations, transfers, maternity, paternity, or medical leave are all situations that you can plan your resources around. So, is it our goal to prevent all turnover? Of course not; some turnover is good. It allows us to right-size the workforce when needed, weed out low performers, and trade up for talent when required. The fact is that turnover can be healthy for the company to maintain a productive workforce.

Unplanned turnover is like the situation we explained earlier, when one of your employees, often the most talented, has quit or taken an unplanned leave of absence. So, why is unplanned turnover bad? Well, it frequently can catch you off guard; you haven't prepared or planned to lose the talent.

So, returning to that highly sensitive word, is there a cost of turnover? Here are just a few of the intangible costs: terminations, recruiting/hiring, low productivity, decrease in overall morale, potential risk of losing customers, loss of institutional knowledge, and even for those newly hired employees, an increase in the unplanned turnover rate may even start to have them gauge if your department/ organization is a beneficial place to work.

Research has shown that the average cost to replace an employee can range from 50 percent to 150 percent of that employee's annual salary. Assuming an employee makes $80K a year, that could cost your organization anywhere between $40K and $120K to replace that position, factoring in all the costs previously mentioned. For those leaders who don't think losing a talented employee occasionally is a big deal, think again. I don't know about you, but I would be worried about my job if I were making six-figure "mistakes" in my department based on my leadership. The fact is, turnover impacts the bottom line, which impacts you!

Why People Leave

We must recognize that each employee may leave for many reasons. In our research and the hundreds of leadership courses we have delivered, often the question is asked: Why did the employee choose to leave? According to "Great Resignation: Survey Finds 1 in 3 Are Considering Quitting Their Jobs," the number one reason people quit their jobs is a toxic company culture (62 percent) that managers often create and enable. While a low salary (59 percent) came in second, remember that the key word here is *low*, not necessarily a fair salary. The rankings were followed by "poor management (56 percent), a lack of healthy work-life balance (49 percent), no remote work options (43 percent), burnout (42 percent), not allowing flexible schedules (41 percent) and limited advancement opportunities or career progression (37 percent)."[1] So, let's explore further the reasons why most employees resign.

Often, the most go-to answer is "They left for more money." While money is often in the top three of lists, it's more based on low salaries, not fair pay. When leaving one organization for another, most employees leave for anywhere between 10 percent to 20 percent of their base salary. Therefore, while the financial increase is of value, it often becomes the final factor in making the rational and logical decision to depart. However, when you think about what motivates an employee to return that headhunter call or explore opportunities online, more money is hardly the number one reason.

As we referenced in Chapter 1, the author Marcus Buckingham said in his book *First Break All The Rules*, "People don't leave companies; they leave managers. So much money has been thrown at the challenge of keeping good people, in the form of better pay, better perks, and better training, when in the end, turnover is mostly a manager issue."[2] Rarely are employees turning in their resignations because they disagree with the strategic decisions made at the board level. The truth of the matter is that they aren't leaving the organization; they are leaving their boss who has a blind spot regarding their needs. Believe it or not, employees are four times more likely to leave an organization due to working for a poor manager than for leaving because of wanting more compensation, better benefits such as time off, a larger role, or increased job responsibility. According to a 2018 TinyPulse Employee Retention Report, "40 percent of employees who don't rate their supervisor's performance highly have interviewed for a new job in the last three months—compared to just 10 percent for those who rate their supervisor highly."[3]

Leaders who aren't kept to a high standard can negatively affect their teams and result in high turnover—even for your best employees. While you have already seen the statistics from our study, additional studies continue to validate the same fact. According to Udemy, nearly half of the employees said they'd quit a job because of a bad manager.[4] Moreover, 56 percent think managers are promoted prematurely, and 60 percent think managers need managerial training.

Top Reasons Employees Choose to Leave[5]

- The employee is receiving too little coaching and feedback.

- The employee has too few growth and advancement opportunities.

- The employee feels devalued and unrecognized.

- The employee is stressed from overwork and lack of work-life balance.

- The employee has lost trust and confidence in senior leadership.

What Can You Do?

Here are three important steps you can take to reduce employee turnover:

- Oversee retention
- Identify who might be at risk
- Choose your talent wisely

OVERSEE RETENTION

It's important to remember that as a leader, you often have much more control than you think regarding "being in charge of retention."

Here are a few essential things to offer when looking to meet your employees' greatest needs:

- Challenging and meaningful work
- Chances to learn and grow
- Great coworkers
- Recognition
- Respect
- Be a great boss—employees want to feel challenged

IDENTIFY WHO MIGHT BE AT RISK

There are many ways to identify if your employees are at risk. The most important one is knowing your employees. When sitting down with leaders, we often ask them how well they know their employees. When they say they know them, we like to test that theory by asking them how well they know their employees personally and professionally. Personal questions include what they did this past weekend, where and when their last vacation was, the current family situation, names, ages, high school or college children, and what is important in their lives.

At this point, we often get leaders giving us a puzzled look. *Why should I know the answer to these questions and why this is important?* Please remember that the questions posed aren't about trying to pry, breach personal confidentiality, or getting you in trouble with your Human Resources department. In fact, we highly encourage you *not* to run out of your office after taking this self-test and demand that your direct reports fill out answers to these questions. The broader purpose of this exercise is to test the theory of how well you know your direct reports. When you understand your direct reports, you know what makes them tick. In other words, you know their *employee value proposition.*

Employee Value Proposition

An employee value proposition (EVP) is a statement that identifies clear, measurable, and demonstrable benefits employees receive when working for an organization. An EVP is a set of offerings your organization provides in return for the skills, capabilities, and expe riences an employee brings to the organization. While it's essential to recognize that the organization should invest in a strong value proposition, if those don't align with an employee's needs, they most often will seek that EVP elsewhere. The core components of an EVP consist of culture, work-life harmony, compensation and benefits, professional development, and recognition.

CHOOSE YOUR TALENT WISELY

In *Good to Great*, author Jim Collins discusses the metaphor of getting the right people on the bus and in the right seats. Often when leaders strive for greatness, the focus first becomes on what or which path to take.[6] Collins speaks of the concept of "first who . . . then what." It is essential to assemble a team of great people first and then decide on a strategy or vision for the company to make it great. Along with Collin's phrase of "getting right people *on* the bus AND getting wrong people *off* the bus," when it comes to attracting and retaining talent, *A* players want to be surrounded by *A* players![7]

Additional Techniques and Strategies

A simple technique to frequently apply when engaging with your direct reports is to utilize the acronym TRACKER.

TRACKER

- **Thank You:** When was the last time you thanked your direct reports for a job well done? Saying thank you costs nothing and lets your employees know you recognize their work.

- **Respect:** Treat all direct reports with the respect they deserve and respect their diverse ideas and unique perspectives.

- **Actively Engage:** Fully engage each direct report in the work they are doing. Remind them how it fits into the big picture and strategy.

- **Challenge:** Stretch the direct report's skill set and place them in situations where they can learn new skills.

- **Know:** Truly know and understand everyone.

- **Educate:** Develop your direct report, share trade publications and industry networking groups, and send them to training courses.

- **Reward:** This doesn't have to be through money. Find out what the direct reports like: cookies, movie tickets, travel, restaurants, etc.

Ten Retention Strategies

According to Indeed, the number one job site in the world, and a global job matching and hiring platform that helps job seekers find jobs, there are ten effective employee retention strategies.[8]

- Focus on the hiring process

- Offer competitive salaries and benefits

- Provide professional development opportunities

- Train effective managers/leaders

- Encourage a culture of open communication

- Create clear work objectives

- Understand what makes employees leave or stay

- Value a work-life balance

- Bring your values to life

- Recognize achievements and milestones

Winning the war on talent is not just about hiring the best; it's about retaining them and ensuring they are engaged, motivated, and committed to your organization's success. By understanding the strategies around talent retention and the impact of quiet quitting, leaders can effectively retain their talent, improve productivity, and enhance their team and company's success. Remember, the war on talent is not a battle won overnight; it is a strategic mindset, listening skills, and knowing your employees will give you insight or success.

Insights

Your direct reports want you to . . .

- realize they often leave managers more than they leave companies.
- provide an Employee Value Proposition that they can align with.
- get to know them personally and professionally.
- place them in situations where they can learn new skills.

CHAPTER 17

Managing Generations

My manager is so stuck in the 1990s.

In today's modern workplace, one of organizations' most compelling challenges is managing a diverse and multigenerational workforce. Traditionally, the generation theory of thinking about multiple generations in the workplace continues to dominate popular thinking. This model dates to sociologist Karl Mannheim (1952) and assumes that people born around the same time period share similar values, beliefs, and motivations. These groups form four generations, each with unique characteristics. The belief is that understanding and effectively managing these generational differences becomes essential for maintaining a harmonious and productive work environment. Typically, these four generations are categorized as follows:

Baby boomers (1946–1964): Members of the baby boomer generation have a strong sense of purpose and often carry a high expectation of themselves and their peers. Many boomers demonstrate an on-the-job commitment and work ethic that often might be referenced by some as being "workaholics." However, a strong drive and motivator for work isn't the only thing that defines boomers. Keep in mind that boomers often represent institutional knowledge of the organization at which they work. Many are long-standing loyal employees who have worked for one organization for their entire career. Based on valuing years of service and loyalty, these boomers may expect those generations that have begun their careers in the years after them to "pay their dues" before being rewarded or recognized via raises or promotions. As their leader, when communicating with baby boomers, demonstrate a level of focus, process, and structure.

Many of these boomers often prioritize work over their personal life. They are those employees who are frequently the first in the office and the last to leave. Always willing to make sacrifices for the company, the phrase *company man* or *company woman* often came from the boomer generation.

Generation X (1965–1980): Sandwiched between the baby boomers and millennials, Gen Xers have characteristics most represented in the workplace as being independent, resourceful, and adaptable. These deep-rooted characteristics can often be associated to having grown up in the generation where dual working households were much more common. Latchkey kids, as they are often referred, came home from school to an empty house and had to take on some household responsibilities as their parents each finished their workday. While boomers most often sacrifice personal and family commitments for business requirements, Gen Xers value a work-life balance and seek opportunities for personal growth. Gen Xers appreciate flexibility, working independently, and in a post-pandemic work environment, leveraging a remote work setting.

Generation Y, also known as millennials (1981–1996): Along with being the most represented in the workplace, millenials are often viewed as the most complicated to fully understand what motivates them to excel. Many millennials tend to seek the most challenging work provided to them and often prefer to avoid the more repetitive or mundane tasks. While they are more than willing to put in the long hours, they will often seek out a life outside of work, wanting enough flexibility to be able to contribute to their professional and personal commitments.

This generation of workers requires regular feedback and seeks to be involved in work-related decision-making. Unlike boomers, who will take on the work given to them for the "good" of the company, millennials want to know their role in the bigger picture of the organization and how their work makes an impact.

Generation Z (1997–2012): Gen Z is the fastest growing generation, making up more than one-fourth of the US population. Despite having grown up during the Great Recession, it could be assumed that this generation of employees might be more risk averse in career choices and driven by a secure salary given the potential economic impacts their parents may have dealt with in 2008 and 2009. However, they value authenticity, individuality, and companies that demonstrate social responsibility. Gen Z seeks out opportunities for creativity and recognizing their digital skills. Gen Z will often seek meaningful projects and a sense of community. Gen Z expects a healthy work-life blend, similar to millennials. When it comes to learning and gaining knowledge, this upcoming generational workforce will seek various online tutorials for professional development, including more nontraditional sources of corporate learning like YouTube. They tend to leverage social media and instant messaging platforms, such as Slack, when seeking quick responses to questions or problems that need to be solved.

However, as researchers examined the efficacy of generational theory, several questions emerged. For example, is there empirical evidence backing up these generational generalizations? Are they true? The answer to those questions is no. As one looks deeper into generation theory, one sees many learning points. Bobby Duffy, the author of *The Generation Myth: Why When You're Born Matters Less Than You Think*, explains that when people are grouped by specific traits, it creates several misleading beliefs and issues. Additionally, it creates divisiveness and exclusion of people. He clarifies that "The generation we were born into is merely one important part of the story, alongside the extraordinary influence of individual life cycles and the impact of historical events."[1]

Duffy and other researchers suggest that the difference seen in each generation is influenced more by the age of a person and the historical events they experience. Moreover, in 2020, the National Academies of Sciences concluded that "Categorizing workers with generational labels like 'baby boomer' or 'millennial' to define their needs and behaviors is not supported by research and cannot adequately inform workforce management decisions."[2]

There are several other concerns related to the generational model. Some examples include:

- Differences in this country are seen negatively, thereby perpetuating discrimination and several "isms"
- Acceptance of stereotyping (e.g., millennials feel entitled)
- Creation of biases
- Oversimplification of a complex and multifaceted area

Since Mannheim's essay *The Problem of Generations* in 1952, generational theory has been studied by many others over the decades. Building on Mannheim's theory came the works of Norman Ryder (1965), William Strauss and Neil Howe (1991), Glen H. Elder Jr. (1998), and several others. As their theories continued to be refined over the decades, new and different models began to emerge.

The Emergence of Perennials

Fashion and tech entrepreneur Gina Pell was one of the first to refer to perennials, stressing the increasing importance of moving beyond broad demographic categories, as mentioned earlier in this chapter, in an effort to understand each human in a fashion that extends beyond the traditional workplace paradigm of age. As Pell puts it, perennials are an "ever-blooming group of people of all ages and types who transcend stereotypes and make connections with each other and the world around them."[3]

It is becoming more apparent that generational differences are becoming less relevant to organizational, team, and individual performance and success. The factor of an employee's age is no longer a core factor in determining an employee's career advancement. As our workplace continues to evolve through increasing changes in advanced technology and process improvement, employees must continue to keep their skills up to date, building on their personal brand. It is becoming more common to see those employees often referred to in this chapter as Generation Z assume team lead or managerial responsibility much earlier in their career. At times, they manage workforce generations decades older than themselves. In addition, this fluid gig economy also finds many baby boomers assuming entry level roles in new professions as their skills and capabilities have advanced with changing technology and needs in the workforce.[4]

The relevance of generation in the workplace continues to lose importance given that the majority of workers across generations are expressing consistent needs for their employee value proposition to be met. For a moment, let's explore remote or flexible work schedules. The ongoing request for employees to have this workplace flexibility extends beyond what previously was considered only a value for millennials but is now consistent across all generations in the workplace. "A survey launched by the World Economic Forum found that 68 percent of organizations would purposely design mixed-age teams to make full use of their joint potential. However, according to a study by Deloitte, only 6 percent of the respondents agree that their managers are equipped to lead multigenerational teams effectively."[5]

A Developmental Perspective

As mentioned earlier, several contributing factors shape our identities. Everything from the culture one is raised in to major life events to technological advancements influences our thoughts, feelings, and behaviors. That said, every human being, despite the year you were born, has one thing in common: We are human. Instead of looking at the differences (generation theory), let's examine the similarities among all people.

- **Connection:** As social beings, we require connection and meaningful relationships. Communication is the vehicle through which we connect or disconnect with each other.

- **Belonging:** The need to connect requires a sense of belonging. To be part of a family, community, groups, and other networks and associations.

- **Curiosity and Creativity:** We are inquisitive beings who drive innovation and desire to create. Our curiosity is like a spark that ignites our creativity, leading to discoveries and inventions.

- **Trust:** We are hardwired to trust. It's the foundation of all social relationships.

- **The Brain:** It contains our past, present, and immediate future (intuition) and drives our thoughts, feelings, and behaviors.

- **Meaning and Purpose:** People who are clear on their meaning and purpose in both life and work are happier, healthier, and more satisfied.

- **Empathy:** We are born to be empathic as social beings. Empathy drives the connection between people.[6]

The developmental perspective deviates from the generational theory in that the lifespan changes we experience have more to do with age than the four archetype categories. Consider the age-related groups that have been defined: the "terrible twos," "acting-out adolescents," and the "golden years." Additionally, think about your beliefs in high school and how those changed in your twenties, thirties, forties, and so on.

That said, the following breakdown of various age groups identifies common beliefs.[7]

The Twenties

- Considering what they will do for the rest of their life
- Leaving home and exploring new possibilities
- Defining themselves as an adult
- Forming dreams and solidifying values
- Engaging in long-term romantic relationships, getting married, buying a home, and starting a family
- Starting to shape their career
- Maintaining an open mind and being optimistic
- Developing their identity at work and in the community

The Thirties

- Significant personal and professional growth
- Building a name for themselves
- Creating their professional "brand" in the workplace
- Being motivated to climb the corporate ladder or get ahead
- Focusing on adapting and adjusting their careers

- Balancing their personal lives, family commitments, and career responsibilities

The Forties

- Reflecting on what they have achieved

- Letting go of unattainable dreams

- Looking for personal fulfillment through self-reflection

- Handling stress and anxiety due to midlife transitions

- Managing physiological changes such as decreased endurance, illnesses or conditions, menopause, and more

- Dealing with family changes, such as children leaving the nest

- Searching for deeper significance in both work and personal life

The Fifties

- Reevaluating life and career direction

- Developing other interests outside of work

- Playing an important role in the organization

- Shifting focus from competing to connecting with others

- Focusing on redefined dreams and goals

- Developing a desire to give back

- Thinking and preparing for retirement

The Sixties

- Planning for retirement
- Managing health and well-being issues for both the self and family
- Pursuing hobbies and leisure activities
- Addressing and managing financial concerns
- Engaging in volunteer work and mentoring

Senior Years (The Seventies and On)

- Managing health issues for the self and other family members
- Balancing work with health concerns
- Dealing with losses
- Finding and utilizing caregivers
- Addressing transportation issues
- Developing strategies for productivity

Conflict often occurs when we focus on differences between people. However, when we seek out similarities in others, they can serve as a catalyst to bringing people together.

How to Manage and Engage a Multiage Workforce

In our previous chapter, we discussed the value and importance of the ability to attract and retain talent. It's essential to recognize the changing dynamics in the workplace and how generational and age differences can also play a role in capturing and retaining the most talented employees. Two major changes are worth considering. Generational thinking is an accepted practice and will not be easily replaced with a developmental perspective because of scientific evidence. As discussed earlier, the brain is far too lazy to make that happen. As we slowly embrace and implement developmental theory into practice, another significant issue remains; the perception people have of different age groups. A perfect example of this is found in the context of the 2024 election. Prior to the election, eighty-one-year-old President Joe Biden turned the reins over to his Vice President, fifty-nine-year-old Kamala Harris. Why? Because of the negative perception of an eighty-one-year-old running the country. The point here is not to raise a political debate, but rather raise the issue of another human fact: Perception is one's reality. Regardless of the generational or development perspective, managing perceptions is the key to managing, engaging, and winning the talent war.

MANAGING A MULTIAGE WORKFORCE

Today's multiage workforce offers many advantages to employers in terms of years of experience and innovative and creative problem-solving. Please refer to Chapter 3 as it relates to the needs of all employees. Additional suggestions that may be helpful include:

- encouraging a culture of lifelong learning,
- providing flexible work arrangements,
- encouraging knowledge sharing, and

- utilizing a variety of communication channels such as in-person and digital.

As a leader, you should place a high value on age diversity in the workplace when assembling teams. This type of prioritization often comes from the top. Hopefully, your executive team also consists of members of different age groups. We don't want to lose sight of the fact that the hiring process and promotions should be based on talent and ability instead of the number of years of experience or an age range. As discussed previously, seeking different options across all age groups can help formulate strategies for all departments and functions within the workplace. Work teams composed of individuals with various skills and backgrounds help to encourage the discussion of a range of possibilities before reaching a solution that works for everyone.

ENGAGING A MULTIAGE WORKFORCE

As we have learned throughout our book, keeping your multiage workforce engaged and productive is about trust and communication. Here are some ways to ensure every age group feels seen and heard:

- Professional development
  - » Irrespective of age, every leader should actively promote professional development. This not only keeps job skills current, including the latest technology, but also instills a sense of growth and optimism. By investing in professional development, leaders can further enhance their team's contributions and support short- and

long-term career objectives, fostering a positive and forward-thinking environment.

- Flexible work arrangements
  - » The pandemic has taught us that all generations desire more flexibility and autonomy in the workplace. Failing to offer flexible work arrangements risks losing and attracting talent. Flexibility enables employers to reach a wider talent pool, eliminating previous barriers like geographic location, transportation, and work schedules.

- Knowledge sharing
  - » Employees of all ages have a wealth of knowledge to share. Encouraging knowledge sharing across different age groups and experience levels fosters learning and enhances employee engagement. It also creates opportunities for mentoring and collaboration on team projects, fostering a sense of connection and teamwork.

- Make yourself available and seen
  - » Leaders, like most employees, wear many hats. It's easy for leaders to remain in their offices, complete paperwork, participate in meetings, and perform other functional tasks. Yet walking the floor to connect with direct reports and other employees strengthens social bonds and builds trust.

Multiage (or generational) connection in the workplace has numerous benefits. When workers codify people by differences, it fuels divisiveness, negativity, and biases. As we age, perceptions can certainly drive differences; however, this normal and biological development occurs for everyone. Recognizing this reality allows people to re-examine their beliefs and perceptions about what will most likely happen to them. That might just cause a person to experience a necessary and positive paradigm shift.

For example, younger workers might experience a sense of connection and joy working with a seasoned colleague as a mentor. Conversely, consider the learning opportunities an older colleague might experience when mastering elements of social media and other technological challenges.

The benefits are endless. Multiage connections in the workplace promote support, open communication, problem-solving, and overall well-being for all age groups. It's time we let go of our prejudices and stereotyping and embrace the one thing we have in common: our humanness.

Insights

Your direct reports want you to . . .

- respect their age and talents brought to the workplace.

- ensure that everyone understands different communication styles and how they can be misinterpreted.

- place a high value on multiage diversity when assembling teams.

CHAPTER 18

Better, Safer People: The Importance of Psychological and Physical Safety

I would love to tell my manager what I really think.

In one of our workshops, we introduce the concept of *psychological safety*. We sometimes model the behavior to illustrate the learning points. For instance, when a participant asked, "What are some examples of psychological safety?" we sarcastically responded, "What do you think?" The participant was conflicted about how to interpret the response. We continued and asked, "Other questions?" "How does psychological safety affect a team?" Again, "Do we really need to answer that question! Let's move on. Do you have any other questions?" And the learning point was made: dead silence as eyes stared down at the table. A quick smile and laughter helped cut the tension in the room, letting the participants know that we were role-playing our responses. At this point, the transition into the importance of psychological safety in the workplace was made.

Psychological safety has become popular in the past few years since Amy Edmondson, a Harvard Business School professor, published her book *The Fearless Organization* in 2018. It is interesting to notice how differently many leaders interpret the meaning of psychological safety in the workplace. We hear people say, "It's about playing nice, so everyone gets along." Or "We have lost touch with common courtesy and being polite to one another." Those are interesting thoughts, but they do not define psychological safety. *Psychological safety* refers to the belief that openly sharing your thoughts, feelings, ideas, and opinions will not be met with retribution.[1]

The hundreds of comments respondents wrote in our surveys suggest that most people felt psychologically *unsafe* at work. Although that term was rarely mentioned, comments about mistrust, lack of autonomy, ongoing conflict, closed communication, micromanagement, and other negative comments lend themselves to an unsafe workplace. Furthermore, if 60 percent would fire their boss, we can assume that they would most likely not feel motivated or engaged or feel their voices are heard, which are all elements of a psychologically safe environment.

These and other benefits of a psychologically safe culture include innovation, creativity, resilience, and team performance.[2] It was the work of Edmondson and Project Aristotle by Google that linked the importance of psychological safety and teams. Edmondson's early research on the relationship between error-making and teamwork in a hospital opened the door to a better understanding of how a team works together, a critical factor in psychological safety. Edmondson's initial intuitive thought was that a high-performing team would experience fewer errors. Surprisingly, she found the opposite—a well-functioning team experienced more mistakes. Further research found that psychologically safe teams are willing to report their mistakes and speak openly about them to help prevent them from happening again, knowing that by doing so, there would be no fear of blame or reprisal.

We find the interplay of psychological safety and team quality interesting. The importance of working together as a team has been studied for decades. Little debate exists on whether a high-functioning team is related to better performance, engagement, and employee satisfaction. It does make sense that trusting teams feel safe to speak openly about their mistakes and to see this process as a learning opportunity. Many of us have seen or experienced what it's like to work on a dysfunctional team, where leaders try to catch people doing things wrong, where team members blame others, avoid, bury mistakes, and work in a self-protective mindset. A psychologically unsafe culture produces people who play not to lose. In the end, the organization and its customers (internal and external) lose.

When people feel safe at work, their well-being, engagement, and motivation increase. In previous chapters, we addressed burnout, stress, and the lack of autonomy and how they relate to workers' mental health and well-being. Now, think about when you might have asked someone how they feel about their job. Some might say, "I like it; it's OK." Contrast that to "Hey, I love my job!" It's a very different standard, for sure. Now, consider the concept discussed in an earlier chapter that feelings are contagious and how those feelings could affect a team. In a psychologically unsafe environment, the turnover rate is high, and there's a high level of absenteeism and presenteeism (low productivity or performance due to working while being sick). Finally, consider how the negative effects of a psychologically unsafe culture contribute to attracting and retaining talent. A psychologically unsafe culture can be toxic to an organization and its people.

Even though the benefits of a psychologically safe environment are clear, it's not so easy to create. Leaders and organizations have remained blinded by functional fixedness, antiquated beliefs and conditioning, and the brain's natural wiring. Earlier, in discussing the importance of neuroscience, we learned that our brain is wired to keep us safe. When faced with change or uncertainty, the brain interprets it as a threat. Unfortunately, many people respond to these realities by avoiding and denying them.[3] We cannot merely *want it to be*; creating a psychologically safe workplace takes a conscious and mindful effort.

Before discussing what organizations, leaders, and individual contributors can do to create a psychologically safer workplace, we delved deeper to see if a relationship exists between psychologically and physically safe workplaces and the risk of errors and accidents.

For the purpose of this chapter, the term *safety* encompasses both physical and psychological safety. Both aspects of safety are interdependent—they depend on each other. Physical safety refers to protecting workers from hazards, slips and falls, and other accidents. As previously addressed, psychological safety refers to an individual feeling safe to express their thoughts and feelings without fear of retribution. If an organization commits to one without the other, it would be like choosing to walk using only one leg. If an organization wants to foster a safe working culture that reduces errors and accidents and enhances trust, engagement, and well-being, it's critical to integrate both types of safety elements.

In creating a safer working culture, it becomes imperative for organizations to recognize some of the psychosocial factors that can affect workers. A study by Khoshakhlagh and others and described in their 2023 article "Examining the Effect of Safety Climate on Accident Risk Through Job Stress: A Path Analysis," found that organizations can decrease accidents by managing job stress in the workplace.[4] Additional studies reveal the relationship between work conflict and accidents.[5] Other psychosocial issues include work overload, lack of autonomy, and mistrust.

A race car team exemplifies the combined importance of physical and psychological safety. We've worked for the past ten years with Ilmor Engineering in Plymouth, Michigan, a globally recognized provider of high-performance engines that makes engines for IndyCars, NASCAR, Arca, and SRX, as well as recreational marine engines. We had the opportunity to ask the CEO of Ilmor, Paul Ray, questions about the interplay of physical and psychological safety. We discussed issues related to workers' stress levels and how that can affect the safety of the driver, the pit crew, and even the fans. He explained:

> The race team is made up of the ground level of mechanics. The mechanics, like other organizational structures, have a leader, and those leaders report to senior leaders. Together, they build the fastest and safest car possible. It should also be noted that the team leaders are ex-mechanics. They understand the mechanic's

mentality and how difficult and stressful the job can be. For example, the mechanics worked twenty-four hours a day in the Daytona race.

They understand when a mechanic raises his hand and says there's a leak, there is liquid, water, oil, or fuel, for example, where it shouldn't be. The team leader trusts that the mechanic is trying to make sure the car is safe. Every mechanic on the race team is empowered to openly communicate their concerns about an issue or problem they observe to the team leader. Every second counts in a highly stressful moment with the ultimate goal to win the race.[6]

The success that the Ilmor racing team has had over the years serves as an excellent example of a psychologically and physically safe team. During the interview, we wanted to explore if there was a negative incident or example. Mr. Ray shared the following:

There was an engineering leader at our workplace who lacked confidence. They believed that any idea not invented at Ilmor was worthless. Whenever junior engineers suggested changes or improvements, the leader would dismiss their ideas. As a result, the junior engineers became disheartened and stopped sharing their thoughts about issues because they knew the boss would not support them.

This type of environment can limit the ideas of a team that are crucial for fast-paced development and execution. A boss who trusts their team to share their insights and knowledge and permits them to experiment without fear of humiliation or disgrace is critical for ongoing success.

The interview ended with a quick review of the salient points and our final statement. Mr. Ray agreed, "So basically, a psychologically unsafe team or environment cannibalizes innovation and creativity."

The interview with Ilmor highlights a couple of vital points that are worth mentioning. First, stress can lead to errors and accidents, so it is crucial for leaders and organizations to address stress and other psychosocial factors that can act as accelerants for workplace accidents. Second, having a trustworthy leader is essential, as it is the top reason why people would fire their boss. Trustworthiness is critical in creating a psychologically safe team.

How can an organization identify, analyze, diagnose, and solve individual and cultural behavioral and physical safety traits? Organizations need to be prepared to better understand active risk management, safety, and human resource management ROI.

There has never been a better time for organizations to embed a physical and psychological safety culture through actionable data. How do you convert workplace apathy and absenteeism into a workplace of empathy, commitment, and well-being? How do you effectively invite and engage everyone in your organization to become a risk manager? How is it not apparent that risk is every employee's business at home, work, or play, and yet we still leave so much to chance? How do senior leadership reinforce their commitment to corporate social responsibility to demonstrate a workplace culture of transparency and trust?

Michael Schultz, cofounder of Aclaimant Inc., introduced in Chapter 14, explained that change is possible when utilizing actionable data. Better data can and should lead to better decisions. It is time to expand the definition of personal protective equipment (PPE, such as helmets, gloves, safety glasses, etc.) to include psychological safety. Why don't organizations come to terms with why advancing physical and psychological safety will construct an environment that drives a leader's purpose and passion for ensuring a safer workplace?

Human error consistently ranks as one of the major drivers of injuries and accidents in the workplace. Therefore, developing a behavioral safety trait assessment tool that identifies an individual's predisposition to risk could be how an organization introduces the term personnel protective equipment to psychological safety. The opportunity to include and embed proven behavioral science tools with mental health resources will generate key behavioral performance indicators across the spectrum of risk management, safety, and human resource departments.

The number of tools, resources, and solutions to ensure what matters most is readily adaptable to pre- and post-loss workflows and advanced analytic platforms. Schultz is adamant that behavioral assessment data should be incorporated to gain greater insight and visibility into recognizing and rewarding individuals for avoiding and mitigating the certainty of risk.

Additionally, organizations need to raise awareness for personal and professional growth, and they include tools for those individuals who may even accelerate the cost of risk. Understanding and expediting the ability to change behavior is challenging, but it requires that actuarial science, along with behavioral science, drive data science. This becomes a risk management strategy designed for continuous improvement.

The critical question is how an organization, leaders, and employees can create a better, safer culture. We have worked with many organizations over the years, where we find banners on the wall and buttons on shirts declaring their cultural taglines. It certainly looks colorful and meaningful, but far too often, we see employees hiding, faking, and constantly looking over their shoulders for the hammer to come down.

In 2023, the professional consulting services firm Pricewater-houseCoopers (PwC) conducted a survey asking employees if their actions and behavior were aligned with their company's values and directions. Once again, as our survey results indicate, there was a distinct difference between how CEOs and employees answered the question. Specifically, 85 percent of CEOs responded usually and often, whereas 45 percent of employees responded rarely, occasionally, and sometimes.[7]

An organization with an authentic culture that commits to pro-social values and encourages a safe culture that strengthens employee engagement, motivation, decision-making, the ability to attract and retain talent, and innovation and creativity. But there is no one-size-fits-all type of culture. Every organization is different, thereby requiring a myriad of employee restrictions or regulations. For example, a chemical plant may have stricter policies on wearing protective gear and complying with OSHA regulations. Similarly, a government agency that deals with classified information may not be well-suited for a hybrid work model that emphasizes flexibility and autonomy. These are realities that senior leaders understand about the culture they want to create, however, not at the expense of eliminating an authentic and safe culture.

Despite the organization's strategy, requirements, and operational discipline, every organization has one thing in common: people. That said, the following suggestions will help an organization, leaders, and individual contributors create a better, safer culture.

When leaders remove their blindfolds and recognize how the people think, feel, and behave in and about the workplace, they may want to make changes that affect their culture. A good start is to explore Dr. Amy Edmondson's seven questions, found in her book *The Fearless Organization*.[8]

In your organization . . .

- if mistakes are made, are they held against the person?
- do employees feel free to bring up problems and issues openly?
- do employees embrace differences?
- is there an environment that exists without fear of retribution?
- can employees ask one another for help?
- do employees undermine one another?
- are employees' unique skills and talents valued and utilized?

We are reminded of what Roger Penske did on the first day after purchasing Detroit Diesel Corporation from General Motors. The story (as we once heard it) went as follows. He brought all the leaders into a room and stated that the *my way or the highway* culture no longer exists. "We are now Team Diesel. If you have trouble adopting this belief, there is the door, and you can leave now." The story may not be precisely how we expressed it, but the learning point is clear. Leaders need to consistently model the behaviors associated with the culture.

Organizations can also . . .

- advocate that all employees are risk managers.

- use behavioral assessment data.

- provide ongoing technical and human-centric training that supports a safe culture.

- consistently check and recheck if the values and behaviors are embraced by all (climate surveys may not work well due to the company not responding or changing the issues or problems that employees identify).

- provide ongoing communication throughout the organization.

Leaders can . . .

- consistently demonstrate their commitment to a safe culture by establishing clear expectations.

- communicate transparently and collaboratively.

- ask with curiosity instead of telling people what to do.

- be personally accountable when you make mistakes.

- be sure to engage the introverts on your team; they may hold back due to the overzealous extroverts.

- practice the core skills laid out in the past chapters: treat people as Adults, manage conflict, listen respectfully, show appreciation so teammates feel supported, and build RICH trusting relationships.

It is interesting to note that while organizations invest heavily in training and educating their leaders, they often overlook providing human-centric training to individual contributors. While the rationale behind investing in professional development for leaders is clear, non-leaders must also develop their self-engagement skills. It is like one side of a rowing team rowing in one direction and the other side in the opposite direction. We have helped several organizations resolve labor disputes quickly by providing leadership skills and concepts to non-leaders, so everyone is on the same page. For instance, when an individual contributor feels that their boss is speaking to them as a Child, they can respond with "I would appreciate it if you spoke to me as an Adult." This approach helps to remove emotions from the discussion, leading to more collaborative outcomes.

Individual contributors can . . .

- always treat one another with respect and dignity.
- communicate as an Adult.
- create an authentic attitude . . . an attitude with gratitude.
- embrace inclusion and belonging.
- be accountable for your mistake instead of casting blame.
- be a team player.

- manage conflict effectively by understanding that what hurts a relationship more is what's not said.

- be true to your values and principles.

"There is no such thing as mistakes; only learning opportunities" is a mantra that exists in safe cultures. And it's the leaders who create a psychologically and physically safe culture and environment. Throughout this book, you've heard us say, "Your people are always watching you, what you say, don't say, and how you behave." Leaders are role models. That was the same strong message Mr. Penske clearly communicated to the leaders when he bought Detroit Diesel.

Insights

Your direct reports want you to . . .

- provide an environment free of risk and retribution.

- provide a physically safe place to work.

- recognize everyone's voice.

CHAPTER 19

Seeing with Clarity

We are not a number; we are real people!

Theories of management have been studied since the late 1800s. You might ask why management and leadership are so challenging to comprehend. The answer is quite simple, but do not confuse simple with easy. This quote from Rita Gunther McGrath captures the essence of this dilemma: "Organization as machine—this imagery from our industrial past continues to cast a long shadow over the way we think about management today."[1] We would like to change the term *imagery* to *habits*.

There has been a plethora of antiquated habits in management thinking and behaviors for decades. A quick review of the various theories dates to the early 1900s, beginning with Frederick Taylor's Scientific Style of Management. The emphasis focused on systems, production, and the optimization of outputs. In 1932, Elton Mayo conducted a series of Hawthorn Experiments. These experiments showed that job satisfaction increased with employees being more involved in decision-making. Around the same time, Kurt Lewin's research on group dynamics greatly influenced management theory.

The 1950s brought Maslow's hierarchy of needs that focused on how managers view employees' motivation. Influenced by Maslow, Frederick Herzberg's two-factor motivation theory identified fourteen factors that increased job satisfaction and motivation when met. The 1950s and 1960s brought the work of Peter Drucker's *knowledge work* and management by objectives (MBO). Drucker believed that managers are leaders who need to collaborate with employees. Douglas McGregor's X Y Theory gives credence to how employees are motivated. The Gen X employees need more supervision, whereas the millennials respond better to recognition.

As management theory has evolved from a machine-like structure to a scientific human-centric set of principles and beliefs, business authors like Daniel Goleman, Simon Sinek, Adam Grant, Linda Hall, Rita McGrath, and so many more have provided a comprehensive understanding of leadership.

In McGrath's 2014 article, she proposed that America has experienced three stages of management: the 1900s, the mid-twentieth century, and the beginning of the twenty-first century. Her forward-looking vision predicted another era. She writes, "Today, organizations look to create complete and meaningful experiences."[2] She was intuitive in predicting how a worldwide pandemic could influence workers' views of the workplace, including their insistence on hybrid models, better work-life balance, and being treated with empathy and understanding.

For the first time in American history, employment contracts are transforming. Beginning in the Industrial Revolution, workers went to work, put in their eight to twelve hours, left the workplace for home, and returned the next day. Today, organizations offer remote working structures as seen in hybrid models because workers have recognized the value of spending more time at home with their families even though they work virtually. They avoided the miles of traffic to and from work, the enjoyment of spending more time with their children, and other intrinsic, human-centric motivators. Wow—what a concept! And something that Mayo, Maslow, Herzberg, Drucker, etc., brought to our attention decades ago.

A New Way of Thinking

The time has come for organizations to move from the hierarchical, top-down leadership structure where the emphasis is on the bottom line and being merely results-oriented. Do not get us wrong; we are not suggesting that profit and organizational excellence are unimportant. Instead, our experience has shown us that the desired bottom line is achieved when the focus is on behaviors and skills.

In other words, the new era has arrived, where workers' personal and professional needs are no longer binary. Motivation, autonomy, control, and other intrinsic needs cannot be separated from the workplace and home any more than a person would choose to see with one eye. The traditional leader-follower model (when leaders tell workers what to do) has created a vacuum of untapped employee potential.

As psychologists, sociologists, and HR professionals understand, altering a person's thinking and behavior is a daunting task. And yet, it can be done. We have seen this in professional sports when a last-place team quickly rose to a championship team, when "good companies become great companies."[3] And we've seen it when we witnessed a dysfunctional Detroit Diesel Corporation with a 3 percent market share transform itself into a profitable functional company with 30 percent market share (before the Daimler Corporation purchase from Roger Penske). They all have one common denominator: human-centric leadership!

But Does This Affect an Organization's Bottom Line?

You bet it does! Before we provide compelling evidence of how a company's bottom line is affected by human-centric leadership, let's take a closer look at what leadership is. When we teach leadership concepts, tools, and techniques in our workshops, we often hear comments like, "I tried that before," or "Yeah, but—" or "That approach is too soft." We try to provide a different paradigm to offset their way of thinking. For example, we ask a participant in the class how they learned math in elementary school. They explained it required a process of learning and practice, and over time, they mastered the core elements of mathematics. Bingo! The light bulb was soon to illuminate.

The same holds true for leadership. It is not an event where one takes a couple of leadership courses and becomes a proficient leader. It requires learning leadership behaviors and skills utterly different from their technical skill set. As the learning continues, they slowly implement what they have learned in practice. Just as you practiced math, you often came up with the wrong answers, failed tests, and experienced frustration. It is no different as young leaders practice what they have learned. Some learn faster and better than others, and some fall short. However, the key is to recognize that we are students of life, where learning is not an event but a continual process.

Another example is David Marquet's 2015 book, *Turn the Ship Around!* As a captain of a nuclear submarine, he took a crew of 135 sailors who were technically, operationally, and emotionally demoralized and turned them into the number one fleet in the Navy in one year.[4] If this transformation can be accomplished on a nuclear submarine, it certainly can be replicated in less life-and-death environments—like the team you lead.

What Marquet accomplished on his ship was beyond remarkable, and some would say revolutionary. It is understood that shifting deeply rooted paradigms can take months and even years, yet Marquet turned his ship around in one year. Using our language, Marquet created an adult culture on his ship. He did not accept children who wanted to be told what to do; he chose not to give orders and created a collaborative environment of thinkers and leaders (Adults). The good news is that we are beginning to see a new generation of leaders who value a more engaged and collaborative leadership style. We suggest reading Marquet's book to get a full appreciation of the steps he took to achieve success.

Now for exciting and compelling evidence from the McKinsey Global Institute 2023 Report, "Performance Through People: Transforming Human Capital into Competitive Advantage." This extremely robust study analyzed 1,800 large companies across fifteen countries. They created four categories into which a company would fall, and they examined "human capital development" and "financial performance."

The four categories are:[5]

- **Performance-Driven Companies**: Focus is on profits and bottom line; goal-oriented; top-down model

- **People + Performance (P+P) Companies**: Focus is on both people and the performance of the company; collaborative, challenging, nurturing

- **People-Driven Companies**: Focused on people; caring, encouraging, nurturing; loses sight of the company's overall performance

- **Typical Performing Companies**: No clear pattern observed

Spoiler alert if you want to read the full report: People + Performance (P+P) companies outperformed all other categorized companies in every metric.

Highlights show that People + Performance companies . . .

- were 4.3 times more likely than the average company to maintain top-tier financial performance for nine out of ten years.

- were two times faster in growing revenue during the pandemic than Performance-Driven companies.

- proved more consistent and resilient compared to other categorized companies.

- generated more significant payoffs for employees, which help retain and attract talent.

- provided seventy-four hours of training per employee.

Change, as we know it, does not come easy. What is easy to accept is complacency and maintaining an attitude of "that's how things are done around here." Yet, the McKinsey 2023 report makes a very compelling argument and shows the need for what leaders and organizations must do to maintain a competitive advantage.

Other than complacency, why do leaders remain blind to what employees are saying despite the evidence from our research, decades of behavioral and psychological theories, and the McKinsey report? As suggested in *Psychology Today*, maybe these cognitive blind spots are a result of what psychologist Daryl Van Tongeren from Hope College calls the lack of "intellectual humility," being open to the fact that we can always learn something from others and be open to the fact that what we know may be wrong.[6] Or, as philosopher Michael Patrick Lynch from the University of Connecticut calls "intellectual arrogance," the refusal to entertain other viewpoints, ideas, or theories.[7]

Putting This into Practice

Before leaving this chapter, we want to add a few elements to our list of what leaders can do to create a more human-centric P+P company:

- Provide ongoing training and development of your leaders. They are the backbone of your company.

- Get all employees involved in the vision, processes, change management, etc. People will feel a sense of ownership and loyalty when their voices are heard.

- Employees need and want autonomy. Allow people to try

new things and make decisions without micromanaging them.

- Incorporate bottom-up innovation and collaboration. Unfortunately, employees are so tied up with everyday tasks that there is no time for innovative thinking and ongoing collaboration. Rethink ways to create time for creative thinking and innovation. This enhances a person's sense of work purpose and meaning.

Perhaps the first step for you has occurred: self-awareness, being mindful of your leadership style and behaviors, questioning your need for control, identifying the good, bad, and ugly learned from your past leaders, seeing yourself from the lens of your direct reports, and remembering how you wanted to be treated when you were a new employee.

This process is not an easy one. Your humanness will lead you back to the old and easy way of leading people. The key is how quickly you recognize this and get back on the path to success.

This is your opportunity; this is your time. If not now, when?

Epilogue

It has been five years since we began our journey to write this book. It's also been the same five years that COVID-19 struck America, leading to one of the worst health pandemics in history. Like many Americans and those around the world, due to the pandemic, health issues, job changes, and other unforeseen life challenges, this book took longer to write than we anticipated.

The additional time we needed to write this book did provide us with the gift of unforeseen yet valuable insights. As referenced in Chapter 1, we were surprised by the results that four years after our first survey, we found an increase from 44 percent respondents to 60 percent respondents stating that if given the opportunity, they would fire their boss! Yet, based on the instability found globally, in our political arena, inflation, mental health issues, etc., it may not be all that surprising.

Younger Workers Increasingly Value Work-Life Harmony

In previous chapters, we discussed the importance of work-life harmony and the changing needs of employees. Recent studies have shed light on how chronic change resulting in feelings of instability has affected people across America and even globally. In early 2024, Ford Motor Company conducted a survey that found that 52 percent of employees globally (Europe, Middle East, United Kingdom, and others) would be willing to take a 20 percent pay cut for a better work-life balance.[1] A balanced life includes more time for themselves, family, and leisure. The survey identified that the generation most willing to forego a 20 percent pay cut was the millennials (Gen Y) and the youngest generation in the workplace, the Gen Zs.

Remember, for the managers currently reading this, those Gen Y and Gen Z employees will be in the workplace the longest over the next twenty to thirty years! The mindset and attitudes of employees have dramatically shifted post-pandemic. As mentioned in earlier chapters, people embrace their quality of life over the material things money can buy. Without question, we suffer from *time poverty*; workers today want *time affluence*. Maybe employees see more clearly as their existential vacuums lose their luster.

We know that people resist change, or more specifically, losses resulting from change. Neuroscience reveals that the brain interprets change as a threat, which increases a person's stress levels, causing a sense of instability. This instability experienced from the onslaught of changes taking place in America and across the globe is affecting people's mental health and overall attitudes. If instability is defined as a state in which the consequences of a mismatch between an individual's functional or cognitive abilities and the demands of their job can threaten continuing employment if not resolved, it becomes critical for organizations and leaders to recognize and manage these realities.[2]

The good news is that many companies are paying attention. Some are building new alliances with mental health agencies and professionals, making accessing help easier. Others are redesigning jobs to better align with hybrid models. Recognizing that employees demand more flexibility in their jobs and schedules, more and more organizations are accommodating. As one CEO who has been against employees working from home told me in one of our coaching sessions, "Maybe people *are* able to get things done at home." This is after having one of their best years during the pandemic.

Ella F. Washington, PhD, an organizational psychologist at Georgetown University McDonough School of Business, writes, "Research shows that when employees can be their authentic selves, and they can work and play toward their strengths, they're not only happier and feel more of a sense of psychological safety, but also do better work."[3]

Unfortunately, many organizations continue to struggle with the challenges faced by their employees and the overall workplace environment. The pandemic created a reawakening of people's attitudes toward work. Just as the great scholars of the past identified, employees are not motivated by autocratic demands, boring and meaningless jobs, or being a cog in a wheel pushed to produce more profit for a company. The changes resulting in people's work-life routine due to the pandemic allowed the brains of many to readjust, illuminating what is essential for people.

Get Set for Success

Leaders must not rely on revised corporate policies and procedures to increase employee satisfaction and engagement. For leaders, the blindfold must be removed. For many, it requires a significant paradigm shift. Specifically, you want to create an adult environment. It begins when you set up your direct reports for success. This happens when you replace old behaviors/habits with new ones. For example:

- Encourage their thinking and willingness to openly communicate with you

- Create a psychologically safe and risk-free environment that stimulates decision-making

- Give intent promoting direct reports to reciprocate

- Relinquish control by creating a collaborative, participatory environment

- Inspire people's talents, energy, purpose, and creativity

As you share information (not dictate orders), your direct reports take ownership (a shift in their mindset) and begin to think like you, not order-takers. Ultimately, you have a team of insightful thinkers who make things happen!

Acknowledgments

We would like to thank so many individuals who helped to bring this book to fruition.

To Ms. Martha Gelletly for her organizational skills and eagle eye. She was instrumental in taking a jigsaw puzzle of chapters and helping us organize it as a presentable manuscript. To Colin O'Farrell who brought his knowledge and expertise in helping us create and launch our initial survey along with organizing the feedback in a coherent and structured fashion. Dr. Jason Young, our behavioral science expert, allowed us to gain a better understanding of the statistics relevant to the survey data. Mrs. Nancy Jennings, Keith's administrative assistant who helped generate ideas and kept Keith's mind calm. To Dr. Stephen Bertman, author and professor emeritus at the University of Windsor, who took the time to provide us with editorial feedback, along with agency and publishing insight he has gained from publishing a dozen books, as we navigated this literary world. To Ms. Corinne Smereka, whose creative skills have enhanced our

Participant Guides and PowerPoints throughout the years and is also an excellent facilitator.

Most important, to all our clients, previous bosses, colleagues, and peers we have trained, coached, and consulted over the years who have provided so many of the *realworld* stories and examples of leadership lessons demonstrated throughout this book.

Notes

Introduction

1. Covey, S. (2006). *The Speed of Trust: The One Thing That Changes Everything*. Free Press.

Chapter 1

1. Higgins, C. (Director). (1980). *9 to 5* [Film]. IPC Films.

2. Marcum, D., and Smith, S. (2007). *Egonomics: What Makes Ego Our Greatest Asset (or Most Expensive Liability)*. Simon & Schuster.

3. Wolf, J. "The Costs of Ego." Wolf Motivation. https://www.wolfmotivation.com/articles/the-costs-of-ego.

4. Buckingham, M., and Coffman, C. (1999). *First, Break All the Rules: What the World's Greatest Managers Do Differently*. Gallup Press.

Chapter 2

1. Kotter, J. (2013, January 9). "Management Is (Still) Not Leadership." *Harvard Business Review*. https://hbr.org/2013/01/management-is-still-not-leadership.

2. The Economist Executive Education Navigator. (May 12, 2016). "Your Employees Wish You Were Emotionally Intelligent." Economist Jobs. Retrieved February 23, 2023, from https://jobs.economist.com/article/your-employees-wish-you-were-emotionally-intelligent.

3. Buckingham and Coffman, *First, Break All the Rules.*

4. Carlson, N. K. (March 11, 2020). "With So Many Leadership Books, Why Are There So Many Bad Leaders?" *The Startup.*

5. Maxwell, J. (1998). *21 Irrefutable Laws of Leadership: Follow Them and People Will Follow You.* Thomas Nelson, Inc.

Chapter 3

1. Sinek, S. (November 9, 2017). *Trusting Teams.* YouTube: Home. Retrieved February 12, 2023, from https:// www.youtube.com/watch?v=fYleJ8An -PI&t=28s.

2. Sinek, S. (2014) *Leaders Eat Last.* Portfolio, p. xi.

3. Taylor, F. (1919). *The Principals of Scientific Management.* Harper & Brothers.

4. Lewin, K. (1999). "Socializing the Taylor System." In *The Complete Social Scientist: A Kurt Lewin Reader* edited by M. Gold. *American Psychological Association.* https://doi.org/10.1037/10319–012.

5. Goleman, D., Boyatzis, R., and McKee, A. (2002). *Primal Leadership.* HBR.

6. Maxwell, *21 Irrefutable Laws of Leadership.*

7. Boothby, E., Zhao, X., and Bohns, V. (2021). "A Simple Compliment Can Make a Big Difference." *Harvard Business Review.* https://hbr.org/2021/02 /a-simple-compliment-can-make-a-big-difference.

8. Gladwell, M. (2019). *Blink: The Power of Thinking Without Thinking.* Back Bay Books/Little, Brown & Company.

Chapter 4

1. Swart, T., Chisholm, K., and Brown, P. (2015). *Neuroscience for Leadership: Harnessing the Brain Gain Advantage.* Palgrave Macmillan.

2. Carroll, P. B., and Mui, C. (2009). *Billion Dollar Lessons: What You Can Learn from the Most Inexcusable Business Failures of the Last 25 Years.* Penguin.

3. Lieberman, M. D., Eisenberger, N. I., Crocket, M. J., Tom, S. M., Pfeifer, J. H., and Way, B. M. (2007). "Putting Feelings into Words." *Psychological Science.* https://doi.org/10.1111/j.1467-9280.2007.01916.x

4. Eisenberger, N. (February/March, 2012). "The Neural Bases of Social Pain Evidence for Shared Representations with Physical Pain." *Psychosomatic Medicine* 74 (2): 126–135. https://doi.org/10.1097/PSY.0b013e3182464dd1.

5. Eisenberger, "Neural Bases."

6. Dewall, C. N., Macdonald, G., Webster, G. D., Masten, C. L., Baumeister, R. F., Powell, C., Combs, D., Schurtz, D. R., Stillman, T. F., Tice, D. M., nd Eisenberger, N. I. (2010). "Acetaminophen Reduces Social Pain: Behavioral and Neural Evidence." *Psychological Science* 21 (7): 931–937. https://doi.org/10.1177/0956797610374741.

7. Boyatzis, R. E., Passarelli, A. M., Koenig, K., Lowe, M., Mathew, B., Stoller, J. K., and Phillips, M. (2012). "Examination of the Neural Substrates Activated in Memories of Experiences with Resonant and Dissonant Leaders." *The Leadership Quarterly* 23 (2): 259–272. https://doi.org/10.1016/j.leaqua.2011.08.003.

8. Melwin Joy, M. (September 2, 2018). "The Neuroscience of Leadership." *Pallikkutam*: 57–59.

9. Rock, D., and Schwartz, J. (May 30, 2006). "Neuroscience in Leadership: Breakthroughs in Brain Research Explain How to Make Organizational Transformation Succeed." *Strategy + Business* Summer 2006 (43). https://www.strategy-business.com/article/06207.

10. Rock and Schwartz, "Breakthroughs in Brain Research."

11. Swart, et al., "Neuroscience for Leadership."

Chapter 5

1. Cooper, R., and Sawaf, A. (1998). *Executive E. Q.* Penguin.

2. Roddenberry, G. (Executive Producer). (1966–1969). *Star Trek* [TV series]. Desilu Productions (1966–1968), Paramount Television (1968–1969), Norway Corporation.

3. Momeni, N. (2009). "The Relation Between Managers' Emotional Intelligence and the Organizational Climate They Create." *Public Personnel Management* 38 (2): 35–48. https://doi.org/10.1177/009102600903800203.

4. Bradberry, T., and Greaves, J. (2009). *Emotional Intelligence 2.0*. TalentSmart.

5. Zhun, G., Yuqi, C., and Yayu, W. (2019). "The Influence of Emotional Intelligence on Job Burnout and Job Performance: Mediating Effect of Psychological Capital." *Frontiers in Psychology* 10. https://doi.org/10.3389/fpsyg.2019.02707.

6. Stein, S., Papadogiannis, P., Yip, J., and Sitarenios, G. (2009). "Emotional Intelligence of Leaders: A Profile of Top Executives." *Leadership & Organization Development Journal* 30: 87–101. https://doi.org/10.1108/01437730910927115.

7. Deutschendorf, H. (June 22, 2015). "Why Emotionally Intelligent People Are More Successful." Vunela. https://www.vunela.com/why-emotionally-intelligent-people-are-more-successful/.

8. Albert Einstein; see https://www.humaneffectivenessinstitute.org/.

9. Goleman, D., Boyatzis, R., and McKee, A. (2002). *Primal Leadership: Realizing the Power of Emotional Intelligence*. Harvard Business School Press.

10. Ramis, H. (Director). (1993). *Groundhog Day* [film]. Columbia Pictures.

11. Hodgkinson, S. (2005). *The Leader's Edge: Using Personal Branding to Drive Performance and Profit*. iUniverse.

12. Bagley, M. (2013, December 6). "George Washington Carver: Biography, Inventions & Quotes." LiveScience. https://www.livescience.com/41780-george-washington-carver.html.

13. Bregman, P. (2018). *Leading with Emotional Courage: How to Have Hard Conversations, Create Accountability, and Inspire Action on Your Most Important Work*. Wiley.

14. Video: *Steve Young on the Importance of Accountability*. (2010). Leading Authorities. Retrieved February 13, 2023, from https://www.leading authorities.com/speakers/video/nfl-hall-fame-quarterback-steve-young-importance-accountability.

15. Connors, R., Smith, T., Smith, T. A., and Hickman, C. (2004). *The Oz Principle: Getting Results Through Individual and Organizational Accountability*. Penguin.

Chapter 6

1. Roepe, L. R. (August 18, 2017). "Why Soft Skills Will Help You Get the Job and the Promotion." *Forbes*. https://www.forbes.com/sites/lisaroepe/2017/08/18/why-soft-skills-will-help-you-get-the-job-and-then-promoted/?sh=37dd2ab354b8.

2. Rowe, M. P. (June, 1990). "Barriers to Equality: The Power of Subtle Discrimination to Maintain Unequal Opportunity." *Employee Rights and Responsibilities Journal* 3: 153–163. https://doi.org/10.1007/BF01388340.

3. Whyte, W. H. (1952). *Is Anybody Listening?: How and Why U.S. Business Fumbles When It Talks with Human Beings*. Simon and Schuster.

4. Harris, T. (1967). *I'm OK, You're OK: A Practical Guide to Transactional Analysis*. Harper & Row.

5. Morris, L. (May 16, 2019). "Leader to Leader: Most Essential Leadership Qualities." The Growth Faculty. https://www.thegrowthfaculty.com/blog/leadertoleader.

6. Meyer, D. E., Evans, J. E., Lauber, E. J., Gmeindl, L., Rubinstein, J., Junck, L., and Koeppe, R. A. (1998). "The Role of Dorsolateral Prefrontal Cortex for Cognitive Processes in Task Switching." *Journal of Cognitive Neuroscience*, 10.

7. Zaki, J. (2020). *The War for Kindness: Building Empathy in a Fractured World*. Crown.

8. Behavioral Essentials. (May 21, 2021). "What Are Oprah Winfrey's Behavioral Traits?" Behavioral Essentials. https://www.behavioralessentials .com/what-are-oprah-winfreys-behavioral-traits/#.

Chapter 7

1. Van der Kolk, B. A. (2015). *The Body Keeps the Score: Brain, Mind, and Body in the Healing of Trauma.* Penguin.

2. Reagan, R. (1982). "Commencement Address." Eureka College.

3. Capobianco, S., Davis, M. H., and Kraus, L. A. (n.d.). *About the CDP— Conflict Dynamics.* Conflict Dynamics Profile. Retrieved February 15, 2023, from https://www.conflictdynamics.org/about-the-cdp/.

4. Kohn, A. (1992). *No Contest: The Case Against Competition.* Houghton Mifflin.

5. Brandenburger, A. M., and Nalebuff, B. J. (1998). *Co-Opetition.* Crown.

Chapter 9

1. *Seinfeld*, season 7, episode 6, "No Soup for You!" written by Spike Feresten, performed by Larry Thomas, aired November 12, 1995, on NBC.

Chapter 10

1. Ibarra, H., and Scoular, A. (November-December, 2019). "The Leader as Coach." *Harvard Business Review.* https://hbr.org/2019/11/the -leader-as-coach.

2. Mehrabian, A. (1967). "Inference of Attitudes from Nonverbal Communication in Two Channels." *Journal of Consulting Psychology* 31 (3): 249–252.

3. Dhawan, E. (2021). *Digital Body Language: How to Build Trust and Connection, No Matter the Distance.* St. Martin's Publishing Group.

Chapter 11

1. Zak, P. J. (January–February, 2017). "The Neuroscience of Trust." *Harvard Business Review*. https://hbr.org/2017/01/the-neuroscience-of-trust.

2. Zak, "The Neuroscience of Trust." All research cited in this section comes from this article.

3. Twaronite, K. (July 22, 2016). "A Global Survey on the Ambiguous State of Employee Trust." *Harvard Business Review*. https://hbr.org/2016/07/a-global-survey-on-the-ambiguous-state-of-employee-trust.

4. Collins, R. (October 14, 2014). "Alan Mulally's Management Secret: Peer Accountability." LinkedIn. Retrieved February 16, 2023, from https://www.linkedin.com/pulse/20141014185728-37742152-alan-mulally-s-management-secret-peer-accountability/?trk=mp-reader-card.

5. Covey, S. (2004). *The 7 Habits of Highly Effective People: Powerful Lessons in Personal Change*. Simon and Schuster.

6. Edelman. (January 19, 2020). *2020 Edelman Trust Barometer*. Edelman. Retrieved February 16, 2024, from https://www.edelman.com/trust/2020-trust-barometer.

Chapter 12

1. Kohn, A. (1993). *Punished by Rewards: The Trouble with Gold Stars, Incentive Plans, A's, Praise, and Other Bribes*. Houghton Mifflin.

2. Adenauer, K. (1976). *Loggers' Handbook* 36.

3. Functional Fixedness. *Oxford Reference*. Retrieved February 16, 2023, from https://www.oxfordreference.com/view/10.1093/oi/authority.20110810104943772.

4. Functional Fixedness. *Oxford Reference*. Retrieved February 16, 2023, from https://www.oxfordreference.com/view/10.1093/oi/authority.20110810104943772.

5. Kohn, *Punished by Rewards*.

6. Levy, A., DeLeon, I. G., Martinez, C. K., Fernandez, N., Gage, N. A., Sigurdsson, S. Ó., and Frank-Crawford, M. A. (2017). "A Quantitative Review of Overjustification Effects in Persons with Intellectual and Developmental Disabilities." *Journal of Applied Behavior Analysis* 50 (2): 206–221. https://doi.org/10.1002/jaba.359.

7. Deci, E. L., Nezlek, J., and Sheinman, L. (1981). "Characteristics of the Rewarder and Intrinsic Motivation of the Rewardee." *Journal of Personality and Social Psychology* 40 (1).

8. Branham, L. (2005). *The 7 Hidden Reasons Employees Leave: How to Recognize the Subtle Signs and Act Before It's Too Late*. American Management Association.

9. Maxwell, J. C. (2008). *Leadership Gold: Lessons Learned from a Lifetime of Leading*. Thomas Nelson.

10. Herzberg, F. (1959). *The Motivation to Work* (2nd ed.). John Wiley and Sons Ltd.

11. Herzberg, F. (January, 2003). "One More Time: How Do You Motivate Employees?" *Harvard Business Review*. https://hbr.org/2003/01/one-more-time-how-do-you-motivate-employees.

12. Kohn, *Punished by Rewards*.

13. O. C. Tanner. (n.d.). "A Year of Employee Appreciation." O. C. Tanner. Retrieved February 29, 2023, from https://www.octanner.com/articles/a-year-of-employee-appreciation.

14. Herzberg, "One More Time: How Do You Motivate Employees?"

Chapter 13

1. Madgavkar, A., Schaninger, B., Maor, D., White, O., Smit, S., Samandari, H., Woetzel, J., Carlin, D., and Chockalingam, K. (February, 2023). "Performance Through People." McKinsey Global Institute. https://www.mckinsey.com/mgi/our-research/performance-through-people-transforming-human-capital-into-competitive-advantage.

2. Gartner Research. (December 2, 2019). "Building Inclusive Leadership to Enable Future Success." Gartner Research. https://www.gartner.com/en/documents/3975805.

3. *Nightline*, "The Deep Dive," directed by Smith, J., aired July 13, 1999 on ABC News.

4. Krombolz, S. (December 2, 2020). "What's Holding Inclusion Back? Leaders' Behavior." Chief Learning Officer. https://www.chieflearningofficer.com/2020/12/02/whats-holding-inclusion-back-leaders-behavior/.

5. Maassen, G. (July 7, 2008). *A Peacock in the Land of Penguins*. YouTube. Retrieved February 16, 2023, from https://www.youtube.com/watch?v=hNeR4bBUj68.

Chapter 14

1. American Psychological Association. (2021). *Work and Well-being 2021 Survey Report*. American Psychological Association. Retrieved February 16, 2023, from https://www.apa.org/pubs/reports/work-well-being/compounding-pressure-2021.

2. World Health Organization. (May 28, 2019). "Burn-Out, an 'Occupational Phenomenon': International Classification of Diseases." World Health Organization (WHO). Retrieved February 16, 2024, from https://www.who.int/news/item/28-05-2019-burn-out-an-occupational-phenomenon-international-classification-of-diseases.

3. Weir, K. (2023). "A Pandemic of Burnout: 4 Questions for Dan Pelton" *Monitor on Psychology* 54 (1): 31–32.

4. Barber, H. F. (1992). "Developing Strategic Leadership: The US Army War College Experience." *The Journal of Management Development* 11 (6). https://doi.org/10.1108/02621719210018208.

5. Gallup. (July 5, 2023). "State of the Global Workplace Report." Gallup. Retrieved November 16, 2023, from https://www.gallup.com/workplace/349484/state-of-the-global-workplace.aspx.

6. Cirillo, F. (n.d.). "The Pomodoro Technique." Pomodoro Technique: Time Management Course. Retrieved August 5, 2011, from https://www.pomo dorotechnique.com/; Cummings, T. (2011). "The Pomodoro Technique: Is It Right for You?" Lifehack. Retrieved December 30, 2018, from https://www .lifehack.org/articles/productivity/the-pomodoro-technique-is-it-right-for -you.html.

7. Gallup, "State of the Global Workplace Report."

8. Weir, "A Pandemic of Burnout."

9. Weir, "A Pandemic of Burnout."

10. Interview with Michael Schultz, cofounder of Aclaimant, January 18, 2024.

11. Sinek, S. (2011). *Start with Why: How Great Leaders Inspire Everyone to Take Action*. Penguin.

Chapter 15

1. Frankl, V. E., (1992). *Man's Search for Meaning: An Introduction to Logotherapy*. Beacon Press.

2. Frankl, *Man's Search for Meaning*.

3. Frankl, *Man's Search for Meaning*, 122.

4. Frankl, *Man's Search for Meaning*.

5. Frankl, *Man's Search for Meaning*.

6. U. S. Bureau of Labor Stats (2021.) https://www.bls.gov/opub/mir/2021/.

7. Cole, J. (April 6, 2022). "'The Great Resignation'—It's Not About Jobs, It's About Mental Health." Center for the Digital Future. https://www.digital center.org/columns/cole-great-resignation/.

8. Sinek, *Start with Why*.

9. Brenner, G. H. (September 5, 2023). "How to Stay True to Yourself." *Psychology Today*. https://www.psychologytoday.com/us/articles/202309 /how-to-stay-true-to-yourself.

10. Pratt, M., Ashforth, B., Cameron, K., Dutton, J., and Quinn, R. (2003). "Fostering Meaningfulness in Working and at Work." In *Positive Organizational Scholarship: Foundations of A New Discipline,* edited by J. Dutton and R. Quinn. Berrett-Koehler Publishers, 309–327.

11. Abellaneda-Pérez, K., Cattaneo, G., Cabello-Toscano, M. et al. (2023). "Purpose in Life Promotes Resilience to Age-Related Brain Burden in Middle-Aged Adults." *Alzheimer's Research & Therapy* 15 (49) https://doi.org/10.1186/s13195-023-01198-6.

12. Ziglar, Z. (January 1, 1987). *See You at the Top.* Pelican Publishing.

13. Holt-Lunstad, J., Smith, T. B., and Layton, J. B. (July 27, 2010). "Social Relationships and Mortality Risk: A Meta-analytic Review." *PLOS Medicine* 7 (7). https://doi.org/10.1371/journal.pmed.1000316.

14. Palmer, B. (July 6, 2021). "Reconnecting in Person after the Pandemic: It's Complicated." *PCMA Convene.* https://www.pcma.org/reconnecting -f2f-after-pandemic-complicated/.

15. Kannan, V. D., and Veazie, P. J. (2023). "US Trends in Social Isolation, Social Engagement, and Companionship—Nationally and by Age, Sex, Race/Ethnicity, Family Income and Work Hours, 2003-2020." *SSM— Population Health* 21. https://doi.org/10.1016/j.ssmph.2022.101331.

16. Adams, Z. (June, 2023). "The Science of Friendship." *Monitor on Psychology* 45–49. https://www.apa.org/monitor/2023/2023-06-monitor.com.

17. Bailey, C., and Madden, A. (June 1, 2016). "What Makes Work Meaningful—Or Meaningless." *MIT Sloan Management Review.* https:// sloanreview.mit.edu/article/what-makes-work-meaningful-or-meaningless/.

18. Bailey and Madden, "What Makes Work Meaningful."

19. Luo, Y., Zhang, Z., Chen, Q., Zhang, K., Wang, Y., and Peng, J. (December 20, 2022). "Humble Leadership and Its Outcomes: A Meta-Analysis." *Frontiers in Psychology* 13. https://www.frontiersin.org/journals /psychology/articles/10.3389/fpsyg.2022.980322/full.

20. Fallon-O'Leary, D. (July 15, 2021). "Work-Life Integration Is the New Work-Life Balance. Is Your Team Ready?" U.S. Chamber of Commerce. https://www.uschamber.com/co/grow/thrive/work-life-integration-vs -work-life-balance.

21. O. C. Tanner. (July, 2020). "Performance: Accelerated." O. C. Tanner Learning Group White Paper. https://f.hubspotusercontent10.net/hubfs /8011865/MLS_Group_July2020/PDF/White_Paper_Performance_ Accelerated.pdf.

Chapter 16

1. Pelta, R. (n.d.). "Great Resignation: Survey Finds 1 in 3 Are Considering Quitting Their Jobs." FlexJobs. Retrieved February 20, 2023, from https:// www.flexjobs.com/blog/post/survey-resignation-workers-considering -quitting-jobs/.

2. Buckingham and Coffman, *First, Break All the Rules.*

3. TinyPulse. (2018). "2018 Employee Retention Report: The Real Story Behind Why Your Employees Are Leaving for Good." TinyPulse by Web MD Health Services. Retrieved February 20, 2023, from https://www.tiny pulse.com/lt-employee-retention-report.

4. Udemy Business. (2018). "Udemy In Depth: 2018 Employee Experience Report." Udemy Research. Retrieved February 20, 2023, from https:// research.udemy.com/research_report/udemy-in-depth-2018-employee -experience-report/.

5. Li, L. (April 8, 2022). "17 Surprising Statistics about Employee Retention." TinyPulse. Retrieved February 20, 2023, from https://www.tinypulse.com /blog/17-surprising-statistics-about-employee-retention.

6. Collins, J. C. (2001). *Good to Great: Why Some Companies Make the Leap . . . and Others Don't.* HarperCollins.

7. Collins, *Good to Great.*

8. Indeed. (n.d.). "13 Effective Employee Retention Strategies." Indeed. Retrieved February 20, 2023, from https://www.indeed.com/hire/c/info /9-effective-employee-retention-strategies.

Chapter 17

1. Duffy, B. (2021). *The Generation Myth: Why When You're Born Matters Less Than You Think*. Basic Books.

2. The National Academies of Sciences, Engineering, and Medicine. (July 21, 2020). "Categorizing Workers' Needs by Generation Such as Baby Boomers or Millennials Is Not Supported by Research or Useful for Workforce Management." The National Academies of Sciences, Engineering, and Medicine. Retrieved from https://www.nationalacademies.org/news/2020/07/categorizing-workers-needs-by-generation-such-as-baby-boomers-or-millennials-is-not-supported-by-research-or-useful-for-workforce-management.

3. Schwartz, J., Denny, B., Mallon, D., Van Durme, Y., Hauptmann, M., Yan, R., and Poynton, S. (May 15, 2020). "The Postgenerational Workforce." *Deloitte Insights*. https://www2.deloitte.com/us/en/insights/focus/human-capital-trends/2020/leading-a-multi-generational-workforce.html.

4. Schwartz et al. "The Postgenerational Workforce."

5. Johnson, M. (December 9, 2021). "Who Are Perennials and Why Do Modern Organizations Need Them?" HCM Deck. Retrieved March 13, 2023, from https://hcmdeck.com/en/blog/perennials/.

6. Samuel, L. (May 3, 2021). "Why We Shouldn't Exaggerate Generational Differences: Lumping Any Group of People into A Designated Bucket Is Misguided." *Psychology Today*. https://www.psychologytoday.com/us/blog/boomers-30/202105/why-we-shouldnt-exaggerate-generational-differences.

7. Levinson, D. (January, 1986). "A Conception of Adult Development." *American Psychologist* 41 (1): 3–13. https://ils.unc.edu/courses/2020_fall/inls558_001/adultdevelopment.pdf; Twenge, J., Campbell, W. K., Freeman, E. (2012). "Generational Differences in Young Adults Life Goals, Concern for Others, and Civic Orientation, 1996-2009." *Journal of Personality and Social Psychology* 102 (5): 1045–1062. https://doi.org/10.1037/a0027408; Twenge, J. (May 12, 2017). "The Real Truth About Generational Differences." *Psychology Today*. https://www.psychologytoday.com/us/blog/our-changing-culture/201705/the-real-truth-about-generational-differences.

Chapter 18

1. Edmondson, A. C. (2018). *The Fearless Organization: Creating Psychological Safety in the Workplace for Learning, Innovation, and Growth*. Wiley.

2. Gallo, A. (February 15, 2023). "What Is Psychological Safety?" *Harvard Business Review*. https://hbr.org/2023/02/what-is-psychological-safety.

3. *Personnel Today*. (May 7, 2021). "Unpicking the Links Between Psychological and Physical Safety." https://www.personneltoday.com/hr/unpicking-the-links-between-psychological-and-physical-safety/.

4. Khoshakhlagh, A. H., Sulaie, S., Yazdanirad, S. et al. (2023). "Examining the Effect of Safety Climate on Accident Risk Through Job Stress: A Path Analysis." *BMC Psychology* 11 (89) https://doi.org/10.1186/s40359-023-01133-2.

5. Martin-Fernandez, S., de los Rios, I., Cazorla, A., and Martinez-Falero, E. (2009). "Pilot Study on the Influence of Stress Caused by the Need to Combine Work and Family on Occupational Accidents in Working Women." *Safety Science* 47 (2): 192–198. https://doi.org/10.1016/j.ssci.2008.03.003.

6. Paul Ray in discussion with authors, April 2, 2024. All quotes from Paul Ray come from this interview.

7. PwC. (June 19, 2023). "Global Workforce Hopes and Fears Survey." PwC. Retrieved January 22, 2024, from https://www.pwc.com/gx/en/issues/workforce/hopes-and-fears.html.

8. Edmondson, *The Fearless Organization*.

Chapter 19

1. McGrath, R. (July 30, 2014). "Management's Three Eras: A Brief History." *Harvard Business Review*. https://hbr.org/2014/07/managements-three-eras-a-brief-history.

2. McGrath, "Management's Three Eras."

3. Collins, *Good to Great*.

4. Marquet, L. D. (2013). *Turn the Ship Around! A True Story of Turning Followers into Leaders*. Penguin.

5. Madgavkar, A., Schaninger, B., Maor, D., White, O., Smit, S., Samandari, H., Woetzel, L., Carlin, D., and Chockalingam, K. (February 2, 2023). "Performance Through People: Transforming Human Capital into Competitive Advantage." McKinsey Global Institute. https://www.mckinsey.com/mgi/our-research/performance-through-people-transforming-human-capital-into-competitive-advantage.

6. Grierson, B. (July 5, 2023). "Certainty Is a Psychological Trap and It's Time to Escape." *Psychology Today*. https://www.psychologytoday.com/us/articles/202307/certainty-is-a-psychological-trap-and-its-time-to-escape.

7. Lynch, M. P. (2019). *Know-It-All Society: How Dogmatism and Arrogance Are Defining Culture and What to Do about It*. W. W. Norton.

Epilogue

1. Howard, P. W. (January 11, 2024). "New Trend Survey Shows Workers Willing to Take 20% Pay Cut for Better Work/Life Balance." *Detroit Free Press*. https://www.freep.com/story/money/cars/ford/2024/01/11/2024-trend-report-ford-salary-work-life-balance/71963699007/.

2. Phil, M., Gilworth, G., Carey, A., Eyres, S., Sloan, J., Rainford, B., Bodenham, D., Neumann, V., and Tennant, A. (July 3, 2009). "Screening for Job Loss: Development of a Work Instability Scale for Traumatic Brain Injury." *Brain Injury* 20 (8). https://doi.org/10.1080/02699050600832221.

3. Washington, E. (January, 2024). "What's the True Future of Work?" *Monitor of Psychology* 67. https://www.apa.org/monitor/2024/2024-01-monitor.

Index

About the Authors

Keith Levick, PhD, or "Dr. Keith," as many of his clients refer to him, holds a master of social work and doctorate in counseling from Detroit's Wayne State University and has worked within or together with large, medium, and small companies and corporations for thirty years. Dr. Keith is the CEO of Goren and Associates, a professional development, executive coaching, and consulting firm in Farmington Hills, Michigan. He has spent many of his years as a psychologist in private practice. He later transitioned his expertise into organizational psychology and business. Over the years, he has demonstrated his versatility and adaptability by working with a diverse range of organizations, including General Motors, Burns and Wilcox, Schoolcraft College, Mercedes Benz, MGM Grand Detroit, and Freeport Memorial Hospital.

He has written and lectured extensively in psychology and business. Dr. Keith is an adjunct professor at Wayne State University and Lawrence Technological University and has authored numerous professional articles. He lectures on various business-related issues around the country as an invited speaker. Dr. Keith was a regular guest for fifteen years on a local ABC-TV talk show, *Kelly & Company*. He has also served as a local expert for NBC and ABC television and radio.

Author photograph by Focal Point Studio of Photography

Matt Bertman has been passionate about his work in the field of talent management and leadership development for over twenty-five years. As an experienced human resource executive, Matt has specialized in the areas of leadership development, talent management, learning, and employee engagement.

Matt currently serves as the senior director of learning and development for Indeed, which is the number one job site worldwide, with the mission to "help people get jobs." Matt manages a global learning team that develops accessible and empowering learning opportunities to equip "Indeedians" with the knowledge, skills, and resources to innovate and drive sustainable success.

Throughout Matt's career he has worked for diverse multi-industries including Gentherm—a thermal technology organization—and Amerisure Insurance Company, where he was responsible for talent management strategies. Matt helped bring Amerisure's Corporate University to fruition along with driving key strategic talent management and development initiatives.

Prior to joining Amerisure, Matt held the position of national director of leadership development for Pulte Homes, where he managed the implementation of management development programs in addition to creating and disseminating the organization's training curriculum and e-learning capabilities. In addition, Matt established the Institute for Continuous Learning (ICL), at the time one of the premier corporate universities in the automotive industry. Matt also has served as a change management consultant for Ernst and Young.

Matt has been recognized by *Chief Learning Officer* magazine's Learning Practice Awards as a recipient of their Leadership Award. Matt is the author of an ATD (Association for Talent Development) Info Line entitled "How to Partner."

Matt graduated from Michigan State University with a bachelor's degree in American Public Affairs. He also received a master's degree in labor relations and human resource management from Michigan State. Matt, his wife, and children reside in West Bloomfield, Michigan.